Landscaping
with Herbs

Landscaping

 with

Herbs

Jim Wilson

HOUGHTON MIFFLIN COMPANY

Boston / New York

1994

Copyright © 1994 by Jim Wilson

For information about permission to reproduce selections from this book,
write to Permissions, Houghton Mifflin Company, 215 Park Avenue South,
New York, New York 10003.

LIBRARY OF CONGRESS CATALOGING-IN-PUBLICATION DATA
Wilson, James W. (James Wesley), date.
Landscaping with herbs / Jim Wilson.
p.   cm.
Includes index.
ISBN 0-395-62237-9   ISBN 0-395-70941-5 (pbk.)
1. Herb gardening.   2. Landscape gardening.
3. Herbs.   4. Herbs — Utilization.   I. Title.
SB351.H5W52   1994
635.7 — dc20   93-32184
CIP

Book design by Ann Gold
Color separation by Sfera - Milano
Printed in Italy by Sfera/Garzanti - Milano

4   5   6   7   8   9   10   SFE

Front Cover Photograph: © Dency Kane
Back Cover Photograph: © Joe Stewardson/© Callaway Gardens Foundation
Cover Design: Ann Gallager

Frontispiece: Herb gardens are for all-season enjoyment. Russian sage
and purple coneflowers complement the colors of the brick walk and
the mist on an autumn morning.

TO MY GRANDCHILDREN,

WITH LOVE

Contents

 *Introduction*

A Lifetime of Herbs

Memory has a mind of its own. Images come to us unbidden, triggered by signals from our senses, especially from our sense of smell, which carries the strongest and most enduring memories of all. A certain smell — a flowery essence, a noxious odor, or a mouth-watering aroma — opens the floodgates of memory. Close your eyes and think of sage or rosemary, dill or lavender. What comes to mind? To me, sage brings memories of my grandmother, my mother, and her sisters preparing fresh pork sausage for the smokehouse, crumbling the dry gray-green leaves stored in a half-gallon fruit jar. I smell dill and see the yellow flower heads, with seeds just beginning

Ornamental herbs, edible flowers, and annuals thrive in light shade at Caprilands Herb Farm, in Coventry, Connecticut.

to form, displayed prettily among the pickles in Mason jars so many years ago. Lavender recalls the faint, lingering fragrance of the English Lavender soap and hand lotion that my mother used long before I smelled the real thing. Rosemary takes me back to 1951, when I rubbed the resinous leaves of an ancient plant in San Juan Bautista, California.

I smell fennel and am eight years old again, as I was when we moved to the farm of an Italian-born immigrant who had grown too old to work the soil. Along the dusty lane approaching the drafty old house he had a large food garden, fenced to keep out farm animals. The far end was planted in small, red-splashed clingstone peaches with incredibly juicy, fragrant fruits, and one tree of the large, late, bland 'Elberta' variety. The near end was crossed with stout wire trellises of 'Zinfandel' grapes; between them were the remnants of Mr. Franco's herbs and potherbs, growing in black, manured soil totally unlike the native yellow loess.

We had no idea of the names of the herbs until Mrs. Franco paid us a visit. She came over for some grape leaves to wrap around what she translated as "tamales," long patties of rice and ground beef flavored with herbs and steamed. That's when I learned the name of the tall, feathery, yellow-flowered plant that lived over winter in our mild Mississippi climate. It was fennel, and it smelled like the spiral ropes of black licorice we bought at the Saturday cowboy movie serials starring Buck Jones and Tom Mix.

Mrs. Franco also identified the chicory that she and her husband grew both for bitter greens and for roots to dry and roast as a coffee additive. Volunteer plants of dill grew here and there; also sage, as well as the decorative and sweetly fragrant Queen Anne's pocket melon, or dudaim, which we soon found was not edible. There were other herbs, but at the time I was really more interested in the fishing worms that thrived in the rich organic soil.

It wasn't long before most of the herbs disappeared, but not the dill and the fennel, which volunteered resolutely. With five children to feed, Dad plowed the ground between the grapevines and planted the complicated succession of vegetables needed to provide the three

Comfrey, mint, artemisia, and garlic chives mingle attractively in this rustic setting strewn with stones at Caprilands Herb Farm.

kinds we usually had at dinner, our noon meal. Mother continued to grow sage to season our home-produced pork sausage and chicken dressing, and gathered the dill for flavoring pickles. She grew parsley to season potatoes. Fennel continued to grow among the weeds along the fencerow, but I don't believe we ever learned to use it.

The only herb we dried was sage. To keep in our humid climate, dried herbs had to be stored in bottles. We couldn't freeze food then; the refrigerators of the day had tiny freezing compartments that were designed only to produce ice cubes, not to store frozen food. (I had seen refrigerators in town; electric power didn't reach our farm until 1936.) Perhaps most important, our local seed store didn't stock herb plants. The only started plants then available were vegetables: cabbage, tomato, pepper, onion, and eggplant seedlings and sweet potato slips. All were field-grown, dug, and sold in bundles of one hundred severely traumatized plants. We grew our flowers from pass-along "starts," or cuttings, or from seed packets that came as premiums in boxes of oatmeal.

We moved to Memphis when I was a teenager, and Dad continued to grow food gardens, which filled every inch of a vacant lot near our house. Three of us brothers went off to service, and when I returned, the World War II service flag with two blue stars and a gold one had been removed from our window. Dad had cut back on the enormous victory garden with which he had fed the neighborhood while we were away. I saw it only once while on leave, and it contained only the basic herbs. One casualty of that war was herb seeds, which had been produced almost exclusively in Europe until the 1940s.

After the war, I grew a small garden around the nineteen-foot trailer that my wife and I occupied while I was studying agriculture, but it was planted mostly in flowers. Flowers were my way of celebrating peace and expressing my confidence in a better life to come.

Herbs came back into my life when I went to work for a Michigan seed company that maintained a huge trial ground away from its headquarters in downtown Detroit. There the company planted samples of seeds from growers all over the world — row after row of flowers, vegetables, and herbs, grown to be evaluated. The European growers of herb seeds had resumed production, but U.S. seeds-men had also begun producing herb seeds during the war. I was in charge of writing the company's catalogs, and I spent many a pleasant Saturday taking notes on the various trial rows while my children played beneath the great old maples nearby. I tried to look at each plant empirically, but my perspective soon broadened. When I had learned a plant so well that it was etched on my memory, I found myself projecting the image into other situations. "Ah," I would muse, "wouldn't that dwarf marigold look good as an edging in my front yard?" or "Why not use chives to edge my herb bed? They are beautiful in bloom."

At home I had a large food garden at the back of our lot and long rows of annual and perennial flowers along the side fences. Like most other gardeners in the 1950s, I had rather rigid ideas about which plants should go where. Food gardens were for vegetables, temporary beds were for annual flowers, permanent borders were for perennials, and herb gardens were exclusively for herbs. Our lot was only forty feet wide, and I had little space to spare. My herbs were jammed into a narrow bed between the driveway and the foundation of the house.

After eighteen years and moves to Tennessee and California, I changed jobs and found myself traveling extensively in both the United States and foreign countries, promoting a high-tech fertilizer. My job took me into botanical gardens, estate gardens, commercial nurseries, greenhouses, and home gardens of all sizes and designs. One of the benefits of the worldwide travel was my exposure to ethnic foods and their exotic flavors. But foreign travel became wear-ing, and I returned to the garden seed industry, this time in a position that took me to fifty different trial grounds around the United States and Canada.

By then, in the 1970s, herbs had become much more important in fine cuisine and in home gardens. The space devoted to herbs in seed company trials had trebled. Oriental herbs had begun to appear, and ornamental edible herbs such as 'Dark Opal' and 'Spicy Globe' basil had been introduced. Large, diverse herb gardens, attractively landscaped, were appearing in botanical gardens everywhere.

Blue-flowered and silver-leaved plants are placed regularly in this model formal herb garden at Cranbrook Gardens, in Bloomfield Hills, Michigan. Note how the sculpture draws your eye.

This elegant little herb garden features a topiary creation on a plant stand at the major axis.

In an attempt to ride the wave of herb popularity, I decided to start an herb farm to grow fresh herbs and rush-ship them to fine restaurants. By that time I had moved from Illinois to Texas, then to Jane's native South Carolina. We named our enterprise Wilson's Savory Farm. Over the next six years, it expanded to include two large greenhouses, two walk-in coolers, and three acres of manicured herbs. Our customer list spread to include restaurants in Seattle, Chicago, Cleveland, Boston, and Washington, D.C., as well as major cities in the Southeast.

Although I had to direct most of my time toward growing culinary herbs and edible flowers, not a year went by without our trying several new decorative herbs. Jane is an excellent propagator and has a good eye for design and color. In the center of our three-acre herb patch, she and I landscaped a sizable area with medicinal herbs, native American herbs, other ornamental herb species, and edible flowers. It entertained and enlightened our many visitors while we were busy filling orders.

After six years, I found myself pulled away more and more from the herb farm, to work on the PBS program *The Victory Garden,* to lecture, and to write garden books. Out of fairness to Jane, on whom much of the work had fallen, we ceased producing herbs. It was a bittersweet decision, but we found that working long hours in all sorts of weather and going for six years without a break are better suited to the young, who have the requisite strength and stamina.

My perspective on herbs has changed since we grew them on Savory Farm. Although I still grow and use the culinary varieties, now I am more interested in using herbs as ornamentals. And now that I no longer cultivate three acres of herbs but grow them in a special garden and among my flowers, I pay more attention to individual plants and take the time to groom them. When I visit estate and botanical gardens, I head for the herb garden, and I am continually delighted at the landscape effects that can be achieved with these adaptable plants.

I invite you to join me in this adventure and explore with me the many opportunities herbs offer for your own garden.

Board-edged raised beds of herbs and vegetables from the colonial era flank the graveled walks at the Mission House, in Stockbridge, Massachusetts.

Chapter 1

Borders

Herbs are plants that have — or once had — some culinary, medicinal, or other domestic use, as dyes, insect repellents, or scents. Most of them are pleasantly fragrant or strongly aromatic; a few are rank-smelling or have no odor at all. Some of them have been in the flower garden for so long that we have all but forgotten that they were once best known to doctors and cooks. At the garden center, you're more likely to find such plants among the perennials than with the other herbs.

When we think of herbs in a historical setting, the first thing that comes to mind is the stylized, intricate, medieval knot garden, rarely seen today

This California garden features drought-tolerant herbs. Mustard and chicory are going to seed; the massive gray-leaved plant is one of the mulleins.

1

outside a cathedral or botanical garden. Yet herbs are equally at home — and much easier to grow — in a modern flowering border. In fact, with the wide choice of handsome foliage and showy blossoms offered by even a modest gathering of herbs, an herb fancier could easily plan an ornamental border composed exclusively or predominantly of herbs.

Such a border might include such showy plants as the yarrows, bee balm, and lady's mantle; also clary sage, hyssop, calamint, catmint, lavender, and Russian sage, which have exquisite foliage as well as highly visible blossoms in white, pink, blue, or violet. (As I write, a clary sage is just coming into bloom in one of my borders. With its enormous crown of papery white, blossomlike bracts, edged with lavender-blue, it is the belle of the ball.) Ancient medicinal or culinary herbs such as lungwort, musk mallow, dame's rocket, and the astringent bistort can expand your options among the ornamentals. Sweet woodruff, lemon verbena, and the white variety of autumn sage offer fragrance and billows of tiny blossoms that help to weave contrasting colors and textures together.

Traditional herbs seldom need the staking and spraying that highly bred ornamentals so often require. Many are suffused with aromatic compounds that are distasteful to pests. As if these attributes weren't enough to recommend them, these time-honored plants are harvested for their fragrance, culinary uses, crafts, and flowers for displaying fresh and for drying. After all, the native American anise hyssop is no less fragrant in the teacup for showing off its dense spikes of mauve flowers in the midsummer border. And there is nothing quite like a few fragrant stems of garden sage, with its quiet gray leaves and purple-splashed lavender-blue flowers, to complement a bouquet of pink roses and snapdragons.

Designing the Border

A generous border offers more design possibilities than a narrow, cramped strip, especially when it adjoins spacious expanses of green lawn and shrubbery. You can set the style of your border — informal, formal, or somewhere in between — not only with the shape of the

Successful herb gardens offer many pleasing vignettes, such as this landscape of clary sage, fern-leaved tansy, hyssop, and white eupatorium.

Oregano stays low until late summer, when it shoots up erect flowering stems.

beds and their architectural features, but also with your choice of plants. For an informal border, try planting large clumps of bee balm, prairie coneflower, and mountain mint and filling in between them with banks of Russian sage and the colorful agastaches. Or you can impose a more formal, controlled style on long, deep beds by laying out arrow-straight edges with square corners, installing backgrounds of walls or hedges, and arranging plants in symmetrical rows. Lines of white and silver plants, such as the mound-forming artemisias, false licorice, and tansy 'Silver Feather', can reinforce the formal feeling. Where borders are long and straight, lines of blue-flowered herbs such as lavender can alternate with the whites. Repetition is desirable in formal borders; your eye will pick up the pattern, as your feet pick up the rhythmic beat of marches or of toe-tapping bluegrass music.

From summer through fall, the herb border is a glorious place, but if you want flowers in spring, you will have to look for them in another class of plants. The spring-flowering bulbs make ideal companions for herbs, since by the time they have finished flowering, the burgeoning herbs will have filled in their spaces.

In some ways, large borders are easier to design than small ones. But small borders can be charming and effective if you can resist the temptation to fill them with a large variety of herbs. Single plants of different species placed wherever you can find the room will end up looking like a motley collection. Instead, consider small drifts of a few choice or very unusual plants. Florentine iris, the source of orris root, which is used as a fixative in potpourris, can be combined with lavender, so that its off-white blossoms precede the sweet blue spikes of the herb. Small clumps of silvery white lamb's ears look good in small borders, especially against a background of old-fashioned roses. One of the saving graces of herbs is that when they have taken their bow on center stage and are out of flower, they lend a quiet elegance of shape and foliage to the garden.

Whatever the size and scope of your design, it is a good idea to research the plants you are auditioning for your garden and to jot down notes on plant height, spread, flowering time, blossom and foliage color, and preferred habitat, whether moist or dry, sunny or

Creeping white-flowered
thyme and woolly yarrow
border a raised bed.

shady. The litmus-paper blues and pinks of pulmonaria blossoms would look lovely with the dusty blue-green foliage and cherry-red blooms of *Dianthus* 'Tiny Rubies', but they bloom at different times. Professional landscapers test their ideas by sketching out each season on different pieces of tracing paper and laying one piece over another, but if you don't have their patience, it's easy enough to take notes and move the plants around in spring and fall.

However you arrange herbs in your border, leave plenty of space between them to allow the plants to assume their natural form and to permit air movement, which minimizes foliage diseases. In general, place smaller plants toward the front and at the ends of borders and taller species toward the middle and back. In deep borders, the height of the plants should crest and fall at intervals along the border's length so you don't have a top-heavy, hedgelike look.

Suitable herbs for the front of the border include the garden pinks, dwarf feverfew, gray lavender cotton, germander, the cala-

A plant of rosemary in a terra-cotta urn adds height to this brick planter of thyme and variegated golden sage.

8

mints, the catmints, lady's mantle, common chives, the small cultivars of mound-forming artemisias, the creeping thymes, and the compact, fine-leaved basils, such as 'Spicy Globe'.

Behind the front rank, which can be alternately thick and thin in informal designs or straight rows in formal arrangements, you can plant the midsize herbs. A recent and lovely addition to the "must have" herbs of this size is garden sage 'Bergartten'. Daylilies combine beautifully with herbs; the butter-yellow hybrids look especially good with blue and lavender-flowered herbs. (In their native Orient, daylilies were once used primarily as culinary and medicinal plants.) The garden foxgloves and Grecian foxglove are among the best tall, slim, spikey plants for lightly shaded borders and, as a source of digitalis, the heart stimulant, also qualify as herbs. Even today's precocious children will be charmed by the story of how foxy Reynard left his pawprints inside the blossoms of foxgloves.

Tall herbs for the back of the border are few in number but vital

There are plenty of pastel colors in this herb border: woolly thyme, curly chives, purple sage, and lavender.

A prize collection of lavender cultivars in raised, mulched beds is backed up by a deep border of perennials.

10

to visual impact. The now-ubiquitous Russian sage can reach three or four feet in height, as will Culver's root, a native medicinal herb with white flowers. In warm climates, lemon verbena grows to lofty heights; so does Mexican bush sage. Angelica and Korean angelica grow to six or seven feet in fertile, moist soil and throw out great white or purple umbrella-form flowers. Tall, button-flowered tansy and *Achillea* 'Gold Plate' both dry well for winter arrangements.

Experiment. Allow a compact plant like lavender 'Hidcote' or creeping crimson thyme to spill over a brick or stone edging. Root-prune a robust colonizer such as bee balm to direct its underground runners along a zigzag route out to the front of the bed. Position large containers planted with bay laurel, rosemary, or scented geraniums at the ends of borders or at corners as accent points.

Choosing Colors

The simplest approach to planning colors for an informal border is to choose mostly complementary pastel shades and scatter a few vivid or dark colors here and there. A formal style, however, calls for the regular placement of plants of only one dark or vivid color to carry the eye straight through the length of the bed. Either style can benefit from seasonal accents, such as early-planted pale yellow calendulas combined with blue violas or, for fall color, the red-flowered cultivar of autumn sage, which shows off right up to a hard frost.

Bolder combinations of color — louder, more saturated ones — can be surprisingly restful where the sun is intense. There, deep pigments relieve the eye from glare. In late summer, the burgundy leaves of 'Dark Opal' basil and the deep purple blossoms of common oregano make a rich foil for the gold of achilleas.

Happily, only a few herbs, such as safflower, have flowers of the harsh orange that quarrels violently with most other colors. Magenta and mauve do abound, and they too can make quarrelsome neighbors. Yet the many herbs with silver, gray, or white foliage and with blue or white flowers serve as effective peacemakers between colors that might clash if planted cheek by jowl.

Experimenting with Foliage

Though we may live for flowers, we work mostly with leaves in landscape designs; it is foliage that provides the framework for color and texture, and most of the fragrance of herbs is found in the oil glands of foliage. Green is more than just one color; notice its many shades, from the deep green of anise-scented marigold to the yellow-green of lemon basil. Look at lady's mantle; its scalloped, capelike, chartreuse leaves combine nicely with gold and white, colors that seem to glow on drizzly summer afternoons.

Explore silver, bronze, and mottled foliage, and take some risks with a few dark colors as accents. The dark, iridescent maroon leaves of purple beefsteak plant and the purple basils contrast pleasingly with pale pinks, grays, and whites. Korean angelica offers tall, slim, reddish purple stems and dark flowers. Flank it with tall, light green lemon verbena or erect, lacy Russian sage and see how much better the angelica displays. Cooks use spearmint more than any other mint, but gardeners may prefer black peppermint or orange bergamot mint for its purple-green foliage. Place a peppermint plant in a tub against a white picket fence backing up a border, or combine it in the container with a variegated green and white mint, such as the peppermint cultivar 'Variegata'.

Designing for Texture and Variety

Variations of texture and plant habit within your herb border will come naturally; the challenge is to place compatible textures and similar plant habits next to one another. To pose a ridiculous combination, try to picture a huge plant of clary sage, with its massive, rumpled blue-green leaves, surrounded by ground-hugging, fine-leaved caraway thyme. Totally inappropriate! Yet if you were to surround the same clary sage plant with catmint or hyssop, the combination would look good, despite the rather small leaves of the catmint. Other small-leaved species, such as the mints, lemon balm, and the calamints, can tie together plants with larger, more distinctive foliage.

Bulbous herbs, mostly in the onion family, can interrupt otherwise repetitious mounds of foliage with their narrow, erect leaves and often spectacular flowers. Lavender-flowered common chives and white, summer-flowering garlic chives are known to most gardeners, but have you tried society garlic, *Tulbaghia violacea* 'Tricolor', with variegated foliage and lavender flowers? Beautiful, and it blooms all summer long.

Even grocery store garlic can produce a dramatic plant. I have a clump of garlic in my perennial garden that may date back to the original owners of this farmhouse, seventy-five years ago. Every year it shoots up stalks of thin leaves like those of irises and three-foot-high flower stems topped with huge round clusters of purple bulbils. They are pungent, to be sure, but they look good, and they attract swarms of butterflies and bees.

Going Modern

Herbs are ancient plants, but this is not to say that you should settle for unimproved varieties. A great deal of breeding work has been done in recent years to make herb plants more compact and less leggy, to intensify fragrance, to broaden the choice of flower colors, and to increase hardiness. Commercial and home garden requirements are not always the same, of course. A perfumer might prefer a tender lavender hybrid that yields the fragrant oil, while a gardener might like the hardy 'Twickel Purple' cultivar of English lavender better. 'Twickel Purple' is a superior border plant, with leaves that are close together on the stems, giving it a dense appearance, and spikes of a rich dark purple. Similarly, the modern achillea 'Moonshine' is preferred by most herb crafters to the older and more massive 'Goldplate'. One of the few objections to the useful lamb's ears is its insignificant blossoms; choose instead the cultivar 'Silver Carpet', which has larger and showier flowers than the species. And against a clipped hedge or the side of a brick house, where the purple blossoms of prairie coneflower would be lost, use the white cultivar, 'White Swan'.

If you have a border that is large enough to offer different habi-

In the Bishop's Herb Garden at the National Cathedral, in Washington, D.C., a single large, airy plant of Russian sage fills a border from back to front.

tats (high and dry or low and moist, sun-drenched or shaded in the afternoon), try to group your herbs by their site preferences. Though most herbs prefer at least a half-day of full sun and excellent drainage, a few will thrive with more shade and moisture. Any plant with variegated leaves will develop and retain its color variations better if given protection from the afternoon sun. Others that grow better in morning sun and afternoon shade are angelica, the monardas, salad burnet, lovage, the mints, lady's mantle, lemon balm, sweet cicely, Johnny-jump-up, pulmonaria, and the calamints. The preference for afternoon shade becomes an imperative in the lower South and at low elevations in the West.

Dark or subtle colors often benefit from visual aids in shaded areas. Great blue lobelia, first cousin to the cardinal flower, blooms in mid- to late summer, depending on the latitude. Its crisp, lettucey rosettes of leaves push up tall, leafy spikes of blue flowers. Against a dark hedge of yew or podocarpus, the plants would tend to blend in or disappear, but place them against a gray fence or wall and they will stand out from the background.

The brilliant color of crimson creeping thyme is accentuated by a border of newly set-out plants of gray santolina in the Western Reserve Herb Garden, in Cleveland, Ohio.

A neat graveled walk
bordered by lavender cultivars
and gray santolina invites you
to turn the corner and step up
onto the flagstone patio.

Chapter 2

The Fragrant Garden

Fragrant herbs: between the heady sugar-and-spice smell of rose geranium and the savory balsam-resin aroma of rosemary lie the scents of camphor, cinnamon, curry, and honey; lavender, lemon, licorice, and lime; pineapple and vanilla. The garden that includes herbs is a perfume store full of secrets and surprises. Fragrant herbs add a new dimension of pleasure to the landscape, even as they enhance its visual appeal.

Consider bee balm, or monarda. We grow it for its color and form, and for the bees and hummingbirds it attracts. But rub a leaf and the plant releases a strong bouquet of fresh thyme, orange peel, and black tea, evoking long-ago afternoons and cups of Earl Grey. Or cup a spray of cherry-

A heady bouquet of scents awaits you in this mixed border of sweet alyssum, heliotrope, and 'Hidcote' lavender.

19

pie heliotrope in your hands to warm and release its fragrance, and you are transported to some pleasant place beyond the borders of memory. Such is the power of these beloved old favorites to awaken dulled senses and stir up memories of gardens past. Personal taste dictates preference, of course; pungent tansy may invigorate one person but repel another.

Whichever herbs you choose to grow, situate them to make the most of their fragrance. Herbal scents are released by pressure and by temperature. Moderate warmth, light, puffy breezes, and humid air — bluebird mornings, mockingbird evenings, whippoorwill nights — send up a whiff of pineapple sage growing along a walk. A warm breeze brings the smell of mint from a neighbor's garden. On crystal clear, cold, windy days, the volatile oils of herbs remain locked in plant tissues.

We can't do much about the weather, but we can bring people and plants closer together. Set the fragrant herbs where you can touch their leaves or brush against them as you walk along a path. Seats and benches are restful, inviting solutions. On a sunny terrace, put in a hedge of lavender, which smells delightful in and out of bloom, and nestle a chair within its reach. Set a low bench in the mottled shade of a deciduous tree and plant a groundcover of shade-tolerant sweet woodruff all around it. Sweet woodruff can withstand some trampling; when bruised, its dense whorled green leaves and foamy springtime flowers suggest vanilla and new-mown hay. You can use sweet cicely, lemon balm, lovage, monarda, and catnip in lightly shaded areas, and set stepping stones among them to make a path to the secluded seat. Several of the mints will adapt to moist soil in light to moderate shade, especially the round-leaved, bronze- or purple-green orange bergamot mint. Remember that the variegated and gold-leaved cultivars of herbs often show up better in shade than plain greens.

Picnicking on a chamomile lawn is a charming British notion, but impractical in most North American climates. Easier to manage is one small, thick plot of the low-growing, vegetatively propagated 'Treneague' cultivar of chamomile surrounding a birdbath. You can

Imagine the fragrance wafting from this lush border of lavender, ready for cutting and drying, at Filoli Gardens, in Woodside, California.

Sweet woodruff is one of the few ground-hugging herbs that will tolerate moderate shade. At Cranbrook Gardens, it has knitted into a dense carpet beneath an old cedar tree.

spritz the chamomile with water every time you fill the birdbath, and enjoy the sweet fragrance released when you tread on it.

Herb steps and herb seats are another European garden conceit, and these are actually more practical than they might seem. To make a modern version of herb steps, fill a brick framework with gravelly soil and plant it with creeping herbs. The simplest herb seat is a concrete bench topped with a layer of sphagnum moss and soil planted with thyme, which is watered often.

Both steps and seats are designed to lure you to step or sit on herbs to release their fragrance. The same idea applies to borders along walks, where creeping herbs such as caraway thyme, dittany of Crete, and English pennyroyal will release their fragrance under pressure. In a small town garden, you might fill narrow, hard-to-mow panels of soil with fragrant creeping herbs in lieu of grass.

The thymes vary wonderfully in texture, blossom color, and fragrance. You can buy thymes with variegated leaves or golden, woolly, or glossy foliage. The culinary thymes have a slight antiseptic smell, but others smell of lemon, caraway, or oregano, or give off a manly, earthy essence that cologne manufacturers would love to capture.

Raised Beds, Containers, and Enclosures

Wherever possible, lift fragrant plantings to within easy reach for planting, cultivation, and olfactory enjoyment. Terraces and low walls make great sites for planting or setting containers of fragrant herbs to form backdrops for benches. Any variety of aromatic garden sage loves to spill over the edge of a low wall; the tricolor or variegated green and cream cultivars are elegant. Unlike some plants, which shrink from the heat of the sun on stone, many of the Mediterranean herbs — hyssop, lavender, thyme, oregano, and rosemary included — luxuriate in it.

Plants that are fragrant but for some reason awkward to include in a bed often work well in sizable pots, which help to put them within easy reach. Perhaps the ultimate potted herbs are tender rosemary and bay laurel. If you place them in terra-cotta pots, you can enjoy their evergreen foliage outdoors year-round in warm climates and indoors during the winter in hardiness zone 6 and north. Collections of herbs such as cinnamon, lemon, and anise-scented varieties of basil and gatherings of mints, thymes, or scented geraniums can also be fun in containers.

Scented geraniums, silver curry plant, and dusty miller are elevated to fingertip level in this wooden planter box.

Gray-leaved lavender and sage blend their delicious aromas with that of a freshly sheared border of sweet basil.

25

Hanging planters, too, can help surround you with fragrance, and like other container schemes for herbs, they offer practical advantages as well. Cuban oregano can become dirt-stained and battered in ground beds but shines in the protection of a large hanging basket. Another tender plant, false licorice, has small, silvery green, wavy-edged, furry leaves on descending branches and is well suited to overhead planters, where its anise fragrance can drift down.

Enclosing fragrant plantings can also intensify your enjoyment of them. The walled herb garden is an excellent and time-honored way to protect fleeting and delicate fragrances and hold them near. Walls of bricks or laid stone are lovely, as are fences and hedges; they will keep wind from robbing the garden of its perfume.

An informal backdrop of fragrant shrubs and trees often makes a soft green alternative to structures. Several woody plants, including native American species, have such fragrant foliage that they have long enjoyed herbal uses. Carolina allspice, New Jersey tea, benzoin, Florida anise, bayberry, and wax myrtle are only a few of these shrubs. The devout herbalist would no doubt hold that the linden tree, with its sweet tassels of spring bloom, belongs in the garden, since its blossoms go in the teapot. A specimen kept small by regular pollarding would add a continental touch to a large herb garden.

Citrus-Scented Herbs

Many herbs mimic the scent of lemons or oranges and are as welcome in the garden as at the table. Surely the grand dame of the lemon-scented herbs is lemon verbena, with its frothy fringe of white blossoms in late summer and open, willowy habit. Its fountain form helps to unite disparate angular herbs growing nearby.

Lemon balm, a mint family member, is a vigorous spreader with apple-green leaves that breathe a sharper smell, more like grapefruit or limes. It likes damp soil and more shade than most herbs, and is good at holding hands with taller and more distinctive plants. The mint family includes other lemon mimics: lemon-scented thyme, with a smell like grated lemon peel; lemon basil; Mexican giant

Bring fragrance to your doorstep with wooden tubs of parsley, garden sage, gray santolina, rosemary, and scented geraniums.

Sweet alyssum, lavender, and
thyme team with red
penstemon to draw butterflies
and hummingbirds while
filling the air with fragrance.
An old-fashioned bee skep
serves as a centerpiece.

hyssop; and the lemon-scented cultivar of peppermint, to name a few. Lemon grass makes a good alternative to ornamental grasses in landscapes.

Scented geraniums include a complex array of foliage colors and scents, but most cultivars derived from *Pelargonium crispum* have foliage redolent of limes, lemons, or oranges. Other scented geranium species smell like roses, mints, spices, or like the air downwind from a sidewalk fruit stand on a warm day.

Licorice-Scented Herbs

True licorice, the root crop *Glycyrrhiza glabra,* is not particularly ornamental and has toxic properties. Happily, a licorice-like aroma can be found in many other genera. The seeds and foliage of sweet fennel have an anisette odor. With its ferny, bright green or bronze foliage, superficially similar to dill, fennel is a good plant for ornamental kitchen gardens. Anise hyssop, a perennial with dark, gray-green, sweet-scented leaves and violet flower spikes, is delightful in naturalized drifts or mixed with perennials or other herbs. Anise-scented marigold, or winter tarragon, smells strongly of licorice. The hundreds of tiny golden daisylike blossoms that open just before frost are among the best edible flowers. In anise-scented or licorice basil, the basic clove scent is underlaid with a strong hint of licorice.

As more and more cultures add their herbs to our own, gardeners may enjoy more fragrances. Nicotianas such as *N. rustica,* the original tobacco plant, were smoked by indigenous Americans. Even though we now class this species as poisonous, such historical herbs make interesting conversation pieces in a more conventional gathering. Most species of nicotianas are rewarding warm-weather annuals, useful for filling seasonal gaps or open spaces among longer-lived plants. In the old-fashioned evening-blooming species, the sweet, heavy perfume of the sticky trumpets of yellow and white is somewhere between cologne and vanilla taffy. However you describe it, a well-grown plant of tall, fragrant jasmine tobacco is probably worth more than a strict definition.

Chapter 3

Gray and Silver Herbs

No other class of garden plants boasts as many silver, near-white, gray, and blue-green plants as herbs. This makes herbs especially valuable in modern landscapes, where the emphasis is away from brash colors and toward subtle combinations of flower and leaf colors. These "foliage herbs" all bloom, but their blossoms are usually secondary to their foliage in landscape impact. Most of them are long-lived and provide light leaf colors all season long. They can hold their own in or out of bloom. Depending on how you use them, they offer a welcome contrast to green leaves, a substitute for flowers, and a light foil for richer colors.

Gray santolina and lavender in bloom complement one another perfectly in this variation on the silver-blue theme.

Many silver to near-white herbs are coated with fine hairs, which shimmer in the light. This flocking is nature's way of protecting plants from environmental stresses: intense sun, drying winds, dry soil, and summer heat. Other gray or gray-green herbs — garden sage, for example — have pebbled leaves, which also reduce environmental stresses on the plants. Still others, like rue, are smooth and hairless, sharing their bluish coloration, glossy texture, and liking for the sun with succulents such as sedums. These, too, are well suited for sunny climates. All demand good drainage, especially during wet winters.

Talk of gray-leaved plants inevitably brings us to lamb's ears. This long-time favorite is often the first purely ornamental herb planted by herb gardeners. It is easy to grow, durable, adaptable, and reasonably winter-hardy. It weaves its silver leaves and stems through the border, stitching together all other colors. Yet despite its beauty, lamb's ears is not the ultimate herb for foliage impact; others, such as the mound-forming artemisias, are just as easy to grow, suffer less from drought, and age more gracefully as the season wears on. When you look beyond lamb's ears and artemisias for inspiration, check out lavender, thyme, oregano, hyssop and anise hyssop, catmint, calamint, horehound, salvia, santolina, Russian sage, achillea, lychnis, senecio, helichrysum, and dianthus. And don't overlook cooking herbs, in all their variety.

The handsome woolly thyme, like other thymes, makes a felty mat of gray-green that nestles nicely against any golden-leaved plant. Dittany of Crete has creeping fuzzy gray foliage and can be used in walls, pavings, and rockeries. Corkscrew chives have twisted silvery quills. Garden sage hardly needs an introduction. Though common, its gray-flannel leaves and tall spikes of purple flowers mix well with everything, and the plant is long-lived where it is fully winter-hardy. A welcome variation, 'Bergartten', has thick rounded coins for leaves and is more mounding in form than the garden variety.

Silver prospectors might also search for lesser-known plants whose species names include such telltale botanical epithets as *argentea,* which means silver in Latin. Look up silver sage, *Salvia argentea,* for example; it makes an excellent alternative to lamb's ears and

An imaginative blend of foliage textures is displayed in this combination of *Artemisia versicolor* (front), green santolina, gray-leaved blue salvia, and native *Yucca filamentosa* (background).

dusty miller for wavy-edged silver accents in flower beds. The words *cinerea* and *griseus* mean gray; *glaucous* means bluish white; *lanata, villosa, ciliata, hirsutus, pubescens,* and *tomentosus* suggest an abundance of plant hairs.

Plants do not need to be solid silver to give the effect of silver in the garden. The foliage of certain species, especially among the shade-lovers, is spotted, dappled, striped, or edged in silver or white on a ground of green. The silver-spotted *Pulmonaria* 'Mrs. Moon' is a good example; although it does not light up the surroundings as solid silver plants do, it is equally attractive in an understated way.

Bright and Dark Colors with Silver

Victorian gardeners loved to combine silver herbs with red garden flowers such as scarlet sage. Now, thanks to the recently introduced herbs *Salvia coccinea* 'Lady in Red' and *Agastache coccinea* 'Firebird', you can have vivid reds and orange reds in an all-herb border. Red shows up well against green foliage, but spectacularly against silver. A few plants combine silver leaves and red flowers and are always at a premium. Maltese cross 'Grandiflora', opium poppy, and the many species of pinks or dianthus are good examples.

A symphony in silver: 'Silver Mound' artemisia and *Salvia argentea* soften a hard corner line.

If you have tried many of the common silver colors in your herb garden and are looking for something new and different to combine with red flowers, try mountain mint, *Pycnanthemum muticum* or *P. incanum*. The branch tips turn silver in late summer, just in time to set off autumn sage 'Furman's Red' or 'Maraschino'. You needn't stop with just the basic reds and silvers, however; throw in some of the late-blooming violet-blue salvias, such as *S. guaranitica,* and white-flowered fall asters.

Dark colors always have to be used with discretion in herb gardens; they tend to drop out of the landscape at eventide, leaving dark

The intense purple of *Salvia superba* 'East Friesland' stands out from the silver foliage of the old reliable artemisia 'Silver King'.

A white picket fence is a backdrop for lavender, lamb's ears, violet-blue-flowered veronica, 'Silver King' artemisia, germander, and sage. Green tansy in the background sets off the light foliage colors.

36

holes among the lighter-colored flowers and foliage. Among the best dark-leaved herbs are beefsteak plant, garden sage 'Purpurea', cinnamon basil, and Korean angelica. You can also reach into the dark-leaved ornamentals, such as *Heuchera* 'Palace Purple', for somber shades.

Silver and Gold

For a summer scheme that smacks of the herb-clothed hills of Provence and the paintings of Cézanne, try using plants with silver leaves and yellow or golden flowers, such as 'Silver Brocade' artemisia, Jerusalem sage, woolly yarrow, or tansy 'Silver Feather'. Provide purple or blue contrasts with your choice of annual lobelia or blue mealycup sage. For an accent specimen among these, try rue or the white-leaved tree germander, which has medium blue flowers that open where the branches meet the main stem and stand out in startling contrast to the ghostly white leaves and stems. Add a Midas touch to your silver and gold combinations with discrete drifts of golden calendulas or the dainty, small-flowered orange signet marigolds.

Silver, near-white, gray, and blue-green foliage, despite their attractiveness, need to be used with a light touch in landscapes. An all-silver herb border, for example, might seem like a good idea, but once installed it would look washed out in a sun-drenched site. However, if you visualize the light foliage colors as the frame of a picture and the reds and blues, or the yellows and golds, as the color accents, the bones of the composition will fall into place. Then you can fine-tune the picture by adding plants with pastel colors. Or it might suit your tastes to put together your colorful herbs and flowers first and insert silver, gray, or blue-green herbs among them: a tussock of artemisia here, a neat edging of lavender there, a touch of woolly thyme where the edging meets the path, a rear guard of Russian sage peeking over the lower plants. All are finishing brushstrokes that make the difference between amateur hour and design mastery in your herb border.

Garlic chives in bloom, gray-leaved lavender, and silver lamb's ears light up a fenced corner filled with varieties of basil.

Chapter 4

Edging
Herbs

Edging plants provide the finishing touch to a bed or border, tying together the diverse elements and setting off the whole package from its surroundings. Many of the best edging plants of all are herbs. But as with a hedge, the success of an edge depends heavily on a suitable choice of species for the climate and site. Perennials should be fully hardy; winter losses will make gaps. For quick results, or around a kitchen garden that gets plowed up each year, you might want to use annuals.

Consider the overall landscape setting when choosing edging herbs. In a country garden with wide paths, compact nasturtiums, billowing out to

A graveled path meanders like a dry streambed through an informal planting of chives, savory, thyme, and scented geraniums.

41

soften the edges without impeding your passage, may be just the ticket. Around a small city terrace, where space is at a premium, a self-contained herb such as a compact cultivar of winter savory would be more satisfactory.

Many herbs now used for edging came to us through the knot gardens of medieval days. Knot gardens call for small-leaved species of herbs that stay rather short, neat, and dense and can be shaped by shearing. Nowadays we prefer the natural look for edging plants, which spares us not only the labor of shearing but the extra feeding and watering that sheared plants require.

Foremost among the graduates of the knot garden school is upright-growing germander, *Teucrium chamaedrys.* Its fine, delicately toothed, triangular leaves are glossy green with gray-green undersides. Germander grows rather slowly into a woody subshrub that makes a superlative edging. Its rose-pink flowers display well against the dark green foliage. Herb specialists offer dwarf and silver-leaved cultivars.

Another knot garden plant is santolina, which grows larger and faster than germander and flowers more heavily. For an Elizabethan effect, you might alternate gray- and green-leaved santolinas in your edgings. Santolinas benefit from a light shearing, but if left to their own devices, they make a relaxed, lacy hem to beds of herbs, flowery borders, and rose gardens.

The Compact Edgers

Every year plant breeders give us more and more compact plants, a drawback when you are looking for flowers to cut for the house but an advantage when you are looking for edging plants. Among these downsized cultivars, 'Blue Mound' rue makes a show-stopper of an edging with its low habit and lobed blue-green leaves. Dwarf sage, a compact, narrow-leaved gray cultivar, is also a fine plant for this purpose. Try combining the tricolor, purple, and variegated green-cream sages when edging a border.

The lavenders make some of the loveliest edgings you can imagine, but remember that they are native to dry climates and can melt

Edgings of green santolina, lavender, and crimson creeping thyme tumble over gravel and timber steps.

At Cranbrook Gardens, a narrow strip of earth between a sidewalk and a building supports an edging of lamb's ears and clipped boxwood. Espaliered antique roses clothe the wall behind them.

A sheared edging of germander unifies diverse foliage colors and textures: gray santolina, nasturtium, 'Silver King' artemisia, calendula, sweet cicely, and angelica.

down suddenly during hot, humid weather or after intense cold spells. You might want to keep a few plants in reserve, growing in pots or a nursery bed, to transplant if you lose any of your edging lavenders. Among the widely available English lavenders, the hardy 'Twickel' has compact, dense growth, but look also at 'Compacta Bomb' and 'Short 'n' Sweet' for edgings. To encourage symmetrical growth, cut back plants nearly to the crown as soon as you see the first signs of buds in the spring. (But be careful; if you live in a capricious cold-winter climate and cut back lavender too early, a late deep freeze can blast the new growth and kill the plants.)

One of the culinary herbs, salad burnet, shapes up into uniformly mounded plants six to twelve inches high and twice as wide. Its small olive-green leaves have sawtooth edges. When you use salad burnet as an edging, set the plants two feet apart so they can develop their attractive natural shape.

Two plants that are not technically herbs have long been used as neat edgings in herb gardens. Dwarf English boxwood, *Buxus sempervirens* 'Suffruticosa', is hardy through zone 7 and, with protection from wind, into zone 6. The small, dense, upright, evergreen plants have lovely gray-green new growth and assume a round shape when quite small. While box is usually sheared to shape in knot gardens, it can be allowed to develop naturally in edgings. Thrift, *Armeria maritima* (not to be confused with moss phlox, which is also called thrift in the South), makes dense, intensely dark green, perfectly round tufts of grasslike leaves about six inches high. In early summer, leafless stems push up to show off pink puffball blossoms.

Herbs for Informal Edgings

True licorice, lemon balm, sorrel, comfrey, and chives edge a walk between fruit trees at Fetzer Vineyards, California.

The durable, informal edging herbs have a blowzy, unfettered look and a billowy, bouncy habit of growth that goes with gardens that receive little care, whether by neglect or by intent. The pearl-gray dwarf beach wormwood makes a choice edging for well-drained soils or windy waterside gardens. It is often generically labeled "dusty miller," as is the equally desirable 'Silver Feather' tansy, with its finely cut leaves.

Old-fashioned annual mignonette, *Reseda odorata*, a pleasantly fragrant herb, looks like a green and brown Slinky in edgings. It is probably too informal to be used more than in bits and dabs among other, more colorful and controlled edgers.

Edible Flowers

Edgings of edible spring flowers are attractive, but consider them seasonal and temporary, to be supplanted by more heat-resistant edgings come summer. Pull out nasturtiums, calendulas, and violas when they have run their course and replace them with heat-resistant ornamental peppers or, in areas with short summers, with compact asters or chrysanthemums for fall color.

If you are fond of nasturtiums in flower arrangements or salads, try the variegated variety 'Alaska'. It has round, marbled leaves and ball-shaped plants that like to drape over a wall or ease over the edges of walks. If the plants begin to crowd the walk, cut them back and eat the prunings; the foliage has a nippy flavor, like cress.

Culinary Herbs

Some gardeners are reluctant to edge with culinary herbs for fear of disfiguring them by harvesting twigs for the table. But the edible herbs branch quickly and cover gaps caused by harvesting. Lining walks with fragrant edible herbs doubles your pleasure, as the fragrances waft up when you brush against them.

The annual 'Spicy Globe' basil makes a fine edging plant and can be sheared if it overgrows and begins to fall apart. It can be alternated with 'Miniature Purple', an annual that is similar in all respects except for foliage color. Lemon basil, also annual, blossoms much more heavily and grows half again taller and wider than the dwarf, compact basils, and makes an animated, lemonade-scented, combination edging and bedding plant to encircle taller flowers.

Petite sweet marjoram, grown in most climates as an annual, makes a delicate blue-green edging that is best enjoyed on raised beds where the airy plants can be seen up close. Most of the perennial

In this garden, the gray path pulls together the various colors and textures of chives, lavender, yarrow, sage, and rosemary.

oreganos are too robust to use as edgings. The slow-growing and half-hardy golden oregano, however, thought by some to be a marjoram, hugs the ground and could be alternated with a somewhat taller edger such as lemon thyme.

Among the perennials are two herbs that shine in lightly to moderately shaded areas: lemon balm and lady's mantle. If you've never seen the jewels of moisture that collect in the hollows of lady's mantle leaves, you are missing a dewy-morning or misty-day treat.

Common chives are often grown for edgings, alone or interspersed with parsley. Where summers are hot and dry, plants of chives look rather weary by early summer. At that point they should be sheared flush with the ground and fed and watered to bring on fresh new growth. The genus *Allium* is huge, and not all its species are garlic- or onion-scented. Allium flower colors range from purple to golden to white, and flowering times from spring through late summer. Many species are low-growing and could be used as edgings.

On the West Coast, fragrant creeping rosemary is long-lived, drought- and pest-resistant, and understandably popular as a wide-spreading edging. In hardiness zone 6 and north, though, it will freeze out and should be treated as an annual.

Hedges

Herbs are seldom used as hedges except in warm climates where the woody herbs can live over reliably. Erect rosemary; bay laurel; wax myrtle, *Myrica cerifera;* lemon verbena; and Mexican bush salvia are good candidates. None of these is an aggressive surface feeder; smaller herbs can grow fairly close to them without competing for plant nutrients and water. In the north, bayberry makes a tall, fragrant, semi-evergreen hedge.

A few of the herbaceous herbs qualify as material for low hedges, including 'Greek Column' basil and the upright scented geraniums; 'French lace', 'Lemon Balm', 'Lemon Crispum', 'Mabel Gray', and 'Skeleton Rose' would make notable low hedges. Pink-flowered hyssop, *Hyssopus officinalis* 'Rubrum', grows very erect, eighteen inches high but only twelve inches wide. A marvelously fragrant, licorice-scented plant, anise-scented marigold, lately distributed widely, has considerable potential for edges or low hedges. Depending on the length of the season, this herb, also known as winter tarragon or Mexican tarragon, can grow to a height of two feet. Where summers are long, it can be kept low by shearing. It flowers quite late, a few weeks before the first fall frost.

Rose hedges, woven of old-fashioned shrub roses that were once used for flavoring, medicine, and perfumery, traditionally go with herb gardens. Among the most fragrant of these are the moss rose, *Rosa centifolia;* the dog rose, *R. canina;* and the French rose, *Rosa gallica.* Caution: some of the gallicas are low and spreading; others grow to five feet high. The old roses are thorny, but you learn to work around them.

The graceful curve of this dry-laid brick walk is edged with 'Silver Mound' artemisia, pink sweet alyssum, silver-edged thyme, creeping thyme, and lamb's ears. Scented geraniums fill the bed at right.

Chapter 5

Herbs in Walls and Pavings

Herbs and stones go together. Stones absorb solar heat and radiate it at night to speed up the growth of herbs in cool climates. Stones dry off more rapidly than soil and can keep soil from splashing on plants and causing foliage diseases. Large stones laid on top of the soil or embedded in it can accumulate capillary moisture on their undersides and sustain herbs that send roots beneath them. But laying aside such practical considerations, herbs look good in the company of stone pavings or walls and have been cultivated close to dwellings for centuries. It is hard to imagine the wall that is not improved by lavender, or vice versa.

Stone risers break this slope in a Maryland garden into terraces. Herbs are growing happily in the high shade of an old conifer.

One of the most exciting opportunities in herb culture is combining herbs and stones in patios, terraces, walls, and graveled areas. Many herbs actually prefer the alkaline environment of new masonry or a mulch of crushed, egg-size limestone. Stones keep small herbs clean, and niches between them provide planting opportunities that are particularly welcome in small gardens where architecture outweighs vegetation. Whenever possible, use native stone when you are constructing garden features, or brick, if it fits the style of the house. Then, when you add herb plantings, the overall effect will be appropriate to your geographical area and home architecture.

The varied colors, textures, fragrances, and forms of plants lend art and life to what would otherwise be monotonous expanses of brick or gravel. Conversely, a mass planting of one kind of herb can bring together an architectural feature of mixed stone or random colors of brick, just as walls, steps, and walks can organize and unify a disparate collection of plants — a welcome opportunity where you might have little choice but to collect one of each or die of boredom. Urban gardeners might find a checkerboard of culinary herbs and square pavers an alternative to a one-of-each-kind herb menagerie.

Herbs can soften the hard lines of walls, walks, and paved areas. Their fine foliage blurs stark edges — think of what lemon thyme makes of a plain brick walk. Vegetation keeps terraces cooler and relieves the glare of concrete. Overgrowth can camouflage unsightly solutions to a change in grade, where trap rock or concrete block is exposed, and plants add visual interest to the angle where walls enter the ground.

Herbs growing along the raw edges of walks or patios knit together architecture and garden. A low double hedge of *Rosa rugosa* and hybrid lavender around a patio can transform it from a casual seating area to a cozy room.

On this patio, Cuban oregano and woolly thyme are spreading unchecked, but crimson creeping thyme and violets are fighting for territory.

Thyme on the Rocks

There is no end to combinations of thyme and stonework. Hardy and aromatic, the thymes luxuriate on flat rocks, trail over walls, and peek out of stony nooks. And there is no end, it seems, to the cultivars

Drab expanses of gray pea gravel and gray stone walls can be enlivened by containers of herbs. This old plant of rosemary looks right at home in its antique concrete planter.

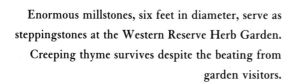

Enormous millstones, six feet in diameter, serve as steppingstones at the Western Reserve Herb Garden. Creeping thyme survives despite the beating from garden visitors.

of culinary and landscaping thymes; more than fifty edible thymes and twice that many ornamental kinds are available through the mail. With their small leaves, graceful habits, and abundant flowers, they are well suited to any garden, from a formal suburban terrace to a naturalized sweep on a rocky bank in the countryside.

One of the best ground-hugging species is woolly thyme. Each spring it grows minuscule silvery leaves and rosy blossoms, and it releases a refreshing green fragrance when bruised. It thrives in a retaining wall or between pavers, and its neutral leaves mix well. Tuck caraway thyme or any of the lemon-scented thymes — green or silver- or gold-variegated — into crevices. Also suitable for crannies are the glossy-leaved, lavender-flowered 'Dot Wells' thyme and oregano thyme, *T. pulegioides,* a mat-forming species with pungent, glossy green leaves and pink flowers.

Most culinary thymes don't creep but grow shrubby with age, becoming broad and spreading. Like sage and lavender, these more upright plants may grow and look better in the deeper soil pockets found between pavers, at the corners of paved steps, on rocky banks, at the bases of large boulders, and in planting pockets dug into graveled areas.

Planted Walls

Walls perform two functions in landscapes. Freestanding walls enclose areas or integrate architectural elements, while retaining walls break slopes into terraces. Whether dry-laid or mortared, freestanding walls offer few or no possibilities for planting, other than as a base for containers. Moss and lichen may colonize these fine structures, but few herbs can take hold in cement until it has begun to crack and disintegrate.

When gardeners speak of growing herbs in walls, they are usually talking about dry-laid retaining walls or high raised beds held in place by stones laid without mortar. These are backed up with soil. Plants inserted into niches in the exposed face of the wall can root into the soil beyond it and adorn its vertical face. Such walls present many wonderful opportunities, both practical and aesthetic — espe-

A terrace paved with bluestone overlooks a secluded arbor. Culinary thyme, crimson creeping thyme, silver thyme, and green santolina plants have been chinked into the spaces between stones.

cially if you plant herbs as the walls are built, so you can provide adequate planting pockets. The terraces formed by a series of retaining walls that have been contoured across a slope also provide excellent locations for landscaping herbs. The same slope would be intrinsically less interesting without terraces, because it would have no vertical planting surfaces and would not be as safe to traverse when planting and cultivating your herb landscape. Steps notched into walls that retain terraces enhance their attractiveness, and can be used as a stage for herbs in containers.

Stick with small plants, either creeping or tufted types, for the vertical faces of retaining walls: blue-gray dianthus, violas, dwarf artemisias, ornamental oreganos, and creeping thymes and rosemaries. Tall, rangy types tend to flop after rains. Reserve them for anchoring the base of the wall, where they won't block your view of herbs that catch on the vertical face. This is just the spot for larger and more upright plants such as garden sage, clary sage, Russian sage, anise hyssop, mountain mint, Florentine iris, and lavender. Then go back and look at where the top of the retaining wall joins the soil behind it. Consider planting mound-shaped herbs at the juncture; they will grow out across the top stones and tumble attractively over the edge. Culinary thymes, upright rosemary, lavender, Jerusalem sage, curry plant, and santolina will thrive in this high, dry habitat.

For yet more variety, combine wall-loving herbs with easy rock garden flowers such as creeping phlox, the sedums, hen and chicks, annual sweet alyssum, and basket of gold.

Raised Beds

Raised beds are constructed to give a welcome change in elevation to flat gardens and to provide the warm, well-drained environment that herbs and rock garden plants love. Most gardeners think first of landscape timbers or old railroad ties for building high raised beds, because of the cost and labor involved in hauling in and laying stone retaining walls. But stone walls, properly equipped for drainage and stepped back slightly for stability, can last forever, needing only occasional repairs to adjust stones that have been pushed out of alignment by freezing and thawing.

Imagine a waist-high, horseshoe-shaped raised bed wrapped around a paved nook containing a chair or a bench. Its unmortared face could be planted with the same herbs that you would use for retaining walls, and a full range of herbs would flourish in the perfectly drained soil of the raised bed. You could easily place annual herbs such as basil, calendula, parsley, and borage in the top of the bed each year without disturbing the rocks and the settled perennials. You might even try the unusual herb black cumin in the warm soil of your raised bed; its seeds are widely used in Indian cuisine. Sitting in the nook, you could reach out and touch the herbs as you relax, see the butterflies and hummingbirds they attract close up, and be immersed in their myriad fragrances.

Whether you plant the vertical faces of retaining walls or raised beds, terraces cut into slopes, steps, or trap-rock faces, you will find that nature will edit and expand whatever you select to plant. If a plant likes a wall, it will cling to it like a barnacle. Hardy, quick growers like calendulas and Johnny-jump-ups will reseed with abandon. One year a plant may disappear from a sheltered niche, only to surface the next summer on an impossible cliff. Not only the reseeding annuals move around; with any luck, your valuable perennial herbs may pop up in unexpected places.

Though most traditional cooking, fragrance, cutting, and tea herbs do prefer sun, a wall can become too hot and dry, depending on its height, the direction it faces, and the climate where you garden. In all but the most northern climates, an eastern exposure, with morning sun and afternoon shade, is ideal for any sort of planted wall. On an exposed west or south face without snow cover, winter sun may warm up and endanger evergreen herbs such as rosemary and santolina, and summer afternoon sun can parch such moisture-loving herbs as lemon balm, sweet cicely, woodruff, and the mints. Even lavender, that hedonist from the south of France, likes an occasional reprieve. Though it recovers with an afternoon rain or the approach of evening, its purple spikes will flag on a south-facing wall at noon.

Decorative stones look good
among herbs. At the
University of California
Botanical Garden in Berkeley,
a lichen-encrusted chunk of
basalt is surrounded by a
silver-leaved tansy,
Tanacetum haradjanii, and
columbine.

Working Paths and Steps

Narrow paths and steps that see heavy use are often at cross purposes with cultivated plants. Most plants find the soil in a path too dry or compacted, or are trampled out. Worse, luxuriant growth can make for slippery going. Creeping thyme and chamomile are the great exceptions. Wherever they can get a foothold at the verges, they make a rather dry, wiry rug, stand up to traffic, and, best of all, release their inimitable aroma when crushed.

If you plan to build steps in your garden, plot an alternate route to the garden's various parts for wheelbarrow access. Design steps to climb, with a comfortable, generous ratio of steps to risers and a dry path through the middle. If you don't use mortar and make your steps wide enough to contain plenty of soil at the sides, those plants that grow well in retaining walls will also thrive here. Imagine a short flight of granite or thick flagstone steps in June, chinked with pinks and dwarf catmints.

Paving Patterns

A checkerboard of large paving stones and squares of soil is a delightful way to organize a diverse collection of herbs, provide a pattern, and restrain underground spreaders such as mint. Try a paved seating area bordered with a checkered edge of squares of tea herbs alternated with twelve-by-twelve paving tiles. Or reverse the arrangement: plan seating at the perimeter of a courtyard or patio and put the checkerboard in the middle. Consider anise hyssop, catnip, chamomile, comfrey, feverfew, horehound, lemon balm, pennyroyal, peppermint, and scented geraniums, but place the big herbs well away from the edges of the squares, so they won't push too far into your seating space.

For accent, place containers of tender herbs on cornerstones — ginger, lemon grass, or lemon verbena, for example. For variety, renew a few squares with different annuals each year. Paved areas are natural for attracting butterflies, which like to bask on warm stones to raise their body temperature. Oregano, parsley, fennel, dill, the gem marigolds, and nasturtiums all attract butterflies.

For a neat edge around your patio, frame the paved area with bricks or the open-centered concrete blocks used for chimneys and plant them with one kind of herb. A fringe of thyme, pennyroyal, chamomile, or dittany of Crete would make a smooth transition between the paved area and the lawn. You may wish to incorporate fancy or treasured pieces — a stenciled block, an old millstone, or an especially ornamental boulder collected on a trip — into the design here and there.

Beautifying Ruins and Blemishes

With age, a mortared wall may crack and shift. You then have to decide whether to point it up, rebuild it entirely, or change it into a picturesque ruin by planting it with herbs. It is difficult to work soil into an existing wall of any height without compromising its strength, but if you have made up your mind to let the wall go unrepaired, then pack soil deep into the cracks and plant them. Use the same sorts of herbs that you would plant on the face of a retaining wall.

Areas where grass grows with difficulty do not need to be blemishes on your landscape. They may be the place for a combination of robust mints and stone. Downspouts are an example; dig out a square of soil, frame the edges, fill the square with coarse gravel, and make planting pockets for a creeping, minty plant such as pennyroyal or Corsican mint. In new housing developments where moist, shady banks have been shored up with boulders or industrial-looking trap rock, conventional landscaping won't work. Instead, find places to fill with soil and turn loose such opportunistic plants as spearmint, peppermint, spotted bee balm, and bugleweed. Plug native ferns into crevices that stay moist; in the Southwest, use cacti and succulents. For camouflage on slopes that are too dry, hot, and steep for grass, kill off the turf and plant such pushy herbs as milfoil, yarrow, tansy, mullein, and the artemisias that spread by runners.

Low garden walls that need repointing, dry wells, crumbling foundations of sheds, disused paths, neglected pools, and so forth are far from hopeless. Shore them up for safety if need be, then use your artistic eye to find planting opportunities for herbs.

Whenever you plant against stone, consider color. Gray-leaved herbs, for example, look good against a dark background. Borage, with its silvery seersucker foliage and pale blue, star-shaped flowers, shows up well against brick. 'Dark Opal' basil, though, might look better against light-colored stone such as quartz or a white stucco wall. New concrete and mortar may of course be tinted to suit your purposes.

Surely there are more stones to turn to find spots to plant herbs and companion flowers. Whatever the scope of your garden, planted walls, paved patios, and graveled areas hold the potential to bring herbs and people closer.

Crimson creeping thyme can take root through cracks, survive being walked on, and bear the heat radiated by paving stones.

Chapter 6

The Kitchen Herb Garden

I n the kitchen herb garden, the first priority is producing herbs for the cook, as well as for the resident flower arranger, wool dyer, and potpourri maker. But practical needs don't have to overwhelm aesthetics. Most people take the time and trouble to devote a garden to herbs because they want a beautiful, fragrant place to pick parsley, braid garlic, bundle lavender, and perhaps escape from everyday demands.

Kitchen gardens are traditionally enclosed by a wall or fence with a gate. While it isn't strictly necessary, an enclosure will not only keep out animal pests but add a look of permanence. Choose material for the fence or wall that is locally avail-

This garden of fragrant herbs, including lavender, pink bee balm for tea, and chamomile, is just outside the kitchen door.

able, reasonably priced, and suited to both the larger landscape and the design of the herb garden within it. You can use wood, stone, brick, or wire fences, so long as they keep the good things in and the bad actors out.

Within the garden, the most frequently used path needs to be quick-draining, nonslippery, wide enough to turn a wheelbarrow around in, and convenient to entrances and herb beds. Construct it of whatever material and in whatever style you like, but crushed pea gravel, fine enough to pack down and not get kicked into the beds, is a good choice for sloping paths. Brick, pavers, or flagstones are also good choices for the main path, if it is level. If you can avoid it, don't build steps into a working garden; they are hard to traverse with carts or wheelbarrows and can cause accidents.

Horticultural literature is laced with plans for traditional kitchen herb gardens. Most boil down to some version of an enclosed square divided into four parts by two access paths, with a simple focal point where they cross. The axis is the logical spot for an ornament or an ornamental planting. It may be a Japanese lantern, a large urn, a sundial, a bee skep, a topiary specimen, a group of herbs in containers, or simply a paved octagon on which you rest your favorite watering can at the end of the day.

In a typical working garden, each of the four quadrants is divided into raised beds, either mounded up or framed in by lumber or bricks. Raised beds can be of any length but should not measure more than four feet across, so you can weed and harvest easily. In the simplest gardens, narrow aisles between raised beds can be either mulched or overgrown with thyme, chamomile, or some other sturdy, low-growing herb.

More elaborate kitchen gardens give you room for a perimeter path and an herb, flower, or small-fruit border between the fence and the path. Formal edgings or parterres of hedging plants give the feeling of a maze as they mature. If you are working with a narrow rectangular garden in which a long path is bisected by a short one, you might place an ornament at the far end of the long path, or set matched ornaments on either side of the entrance or at the ends of

This kitchen garden supplies plenty of basil for using fresh and preserving in oils, wines, vinegars, and butters. The purple and green basils edge tall lavender.

the cross path. In any case, regular and repeated patterns, good-quality structures, well-kept edges, and a single theme will strengthen any design. In long, narrow gardens, a strong longitudinal pattern of bricks or pavers can carry the eye along the length of the garden to the ornament.

What to plant in your kitchen garden depends on your own likes and hobbies. In a large working garden you can group plants according to their major use, having a plot for dye plants, one for medicinal herbs of historical interest, one for cooking herbs, one for long-stemmed flowers and herbs for cutting and drying, one for herbs for scenting and potpourri, and so forth. In a small garden you will be hard pressed to find room for more than two or three plants of each of the major culinary herbs alone, much less herbs and flowers for crafts. If your garden is frequented by small children, it makes sense to exclude plants that are toxic when ingested or that can cause contact dermatitis — castor beans, rue, pennyroyal, and pungent peppers, to name a few.

Culinary Herbs

Whatever their tastes and hobbies, most gardeners want to plant a good supply of versatile cooking herbs. Basil, chervil, chives, cilantro (coriander), dill, lovage, marjoram, oregano, parsley, rosemary, summer and winter savory, tarragon, and thyme will find many uses. Also include herbs to flavor your favorite ethnic foods or fancy cuisines. You can grow garlic and shallots from bulbs, and coriander, fennel, black mustard (*Brassica nigra*), dill, and black cumin from seed to use in Indian cuisine. Cilantro; Cuban cilantro, or culentro, *Eryngium foetidum;* and 'Jalapeno', 'Ancho', and pimiento peppers (chilies) will help to season Mexican and Caribbean dishes.

Asian herbs include such staples as lombok chilies, a variety of *Capsicum annuum;* green perilla or shiso, *Perilla frutescens;* beefsteak plant, also *P. frutescens;* rocambole or serpent garlic; ginger; and lemon grass. Yellow daylilies pressed into white icing on a cake are gorgeous; their buds may be used to make Chinese soups. In a garden devoted to the culture of oriental herbs, you might find it appropriate to use bamboo fencing, gravel paths, carefully placed stones, and a bit of orientalia.

The tea herbs can be used to flavor tea or steeped in hot water to make tisanes. Popular tea herbs include bee balm, lemon verbena, sage, chamomile, rosemary, and of course mint. Besides peppermint and spearmint, look at unusual cultivars such as 'Orange Bergamot', which has large bronzy-purple leaves and the aroma of Earl Grey tea steeping in the pot.

Edible Flowers

Not all flowers are edible; a few are poisonous, some are edible but barely palatable, and some are just as delicious as they are beautiful. Edible flowers make splendid edgings and beauty spots throughout your kitchen herb garden, providing blossoms for bouquets and for garnishing salads, cakes, and serving plates. A few of the best are calendula, chives, garlic chives, nasturtium, nigella, roses, violets, and daylilies. Some of the common herbs and potherbs have tender, delicious flowers that are not ornate but make scrumptious additions to salads; arugula, dill, fennel, and curled cress are a few. The tightly rolled flower buds of the woody shrub rose of Sharon or althea, *Hibiscus syriacus,* are colorful and have a sweet, nutty taste.

Aromatics and Decoratives

After you have planted your culinary herbs, look around your kitchen garden to see if you have a few open spots for herbs that are especially aromatic or useful in arrangements. If not, find space in your flower borders for them. Collect bud vases of various heights and colors and use them to bring your herbs indoors for everyone to enjoy. Keep a drying screen handy for drying blossoms for potpourri, and use a drying rack for long-stemmed flowers. It would be a shame to let the beautiful blossoms of roses, lavender, sage, common oregano, and cinnamon basil, among others, shatter or wither on the

"A little dab'll do ya": the single plant of 'Purple Ruffles' basil is just enough. Beside it are 'African Blue' and sweet basil, and in front are summer savory and curly parsley.

This harvest of herbs can be used for drying, making tea, and flavoring savory dishes and salads. The basket holds fennel, parsley, chives, variegated sage, purple sage in flower, rosemary, and silver thyme.

plant, or to pass up wreath-making herbs such as artemisia, teasel, and safflower.

A Weaver's Garden

If you like to weave, knit, quilt, or embroider, consider experimenting with a selection of dye herbs in your working garden. Most are rather rangy in appearance but can be supported by more attractive herbs and annuals. Madder, *Rubia tinctorum,* is quite easy to grow. Properly handled, its roots yield a red color. The leaves and flowers of lavender cotton, or gray santolina, yield a yellow dye. Woad, *Isatis tinctoria,* colors cloth blue. These are but a few of the numerous dyeing herbs that are easy to grow.

Kitchen Garden Culture

Your first impulse may be to plant herbs together in attractive ways to accommodate their various heights, colors, and textures. But once you have made a preliminary plan, pause and reconsider the cultural needs of each. Most herbs need good drainage and full sun, or afternoon shade in hot climates. Some, such as angelica, sweet cicely, lemon balm, lovage, and the mints, perform better where the soil stays moist. North of zone 7, frost-tender plants should be grown in containers for taking indoors in the fall; rosemary, bay, scented geraniums, ginger, lemon grass, and your favorite citrus trees are among them. Beloved but invasive herbs such as horseradish, comfrey, the mints, lemon balm, and monarda can also be confined in containers or grown within below-ground barriers. Grow bulbous herbs such as garlic and shallots in separate beds for easy harvesting.

At some point in your planning, you may decide to move some of the heavily harvested herbs — basil and such — to your food garden. But the other side of the coin is that some vegetable crops might fare better in your kitchen herb garden. If you till your vegetable garden yearly and have to work around the perennial asparagus, rhubarb, and strawberries, why not move those to your kitchen herb garden, where the soil is worked only when a plant is removed? The

A model kitchen herb garden at Peconic River Herb Farm, in Calverton, New York, features a potted bay tree. Around it grow summer savory, basil, purple perilla, chives, lavender, and thyme.

75

same applies to small fruits, grapes, and hops, which can be trained on the kitchen garden fence. You can use shrub roses and dwarf fruit trees as accent or entrance plants, and they will help create shade if planted on the southern and western sides.

Traditional Themes

If you are fond of the Middle Ages, consider creating a walled kitchen garden, with roses and small fruits espaliered on the wall, a sundial or fountain in the center, and ornamental beds of daisies, pinks, violets, iris, hyssop, and lavender alternating with the culinary or aromatic herbs. A caution about walls: they are advantageous in the North and in windy areas, but in extremely hot climates they should be pierced liberally to allow air to flow through.

If you live in a warm climate and would like a Mediterranean theme, consider growing caper bushes, rosemary, lavender, and basils in abundance, displaying them with white stone and classic urns, including potted specimens of bay, dwarf citrus, or scented geraniums trained into tree form, and training fig trees and grapevines against the fences. A splashing fountain at the axis of the walks would complete the picture.

New Englanders and southerners alike would be at home in a colonial kitchen garden, fenced with picket and planted with medicinal, fragrant, and dye herbs (for the sake of authenticity), augmented with salad and savory herbs. For ornaments, use items that were functional in colonial days — a bee skep, for example.

A Victorian motif may appeal to gardeners who like to put on a great show while literally overwhelming visitors with fragrance. For starters, put in a wrought iron fence and an ornate iron gate, pave the pathways with brick in patterns, and install a rococo fountain that can double as a birdbath, or perhaps a gazing ball. Then, edge herb beds with vivid flowers and back them up with powerfully fragrant flowers such as tuberoses and the evening-blooming white nicotiana. Place tubs of tropical flowers as accent points. Your Victorian garden won't fit today's specifications for a kitchen garden, but your great-grandmother would feel right at home in it.

Author Rosalind Creasy decorates her kitchen entrance with parsley, silver-edged thyme, and 'Spicy Globe' basil in old olive oil and coffee tins, with holes punched for drainage. (Sorry, puss, no catnip.)

Chapter 7

Growing Herbs in Containers

Herbs are uniquely suited to container culture. In fact, it's often easier to grow them in pots than in the ground. They do well in the rather dry, well-aerated, and warm artificial soils used in containers, and they won't grow out of bounds. Even such invasive herbs as mint, bergamot, and lemon balm can be made to behave in the confines of a container. And, of course, containers allow you to place your herbs wherever you want them — where they will get the most sun or be convenient to the kitchen or scent a path or a patio with their fragrance.

Containers of various heights give changes of elevation to this herb and flower garden, which includes petunias, nicotiana, rosemary, white lobelia, lemon marigolds (edible), sweet basil, and summer savory.

Terra-cotta (fired clay) containers have been favored for herbs for centuries: they evaporate water rapidly and their rich red color develops a lovely patina with age. Painted wood containers look good with herbs, as do sections of chimney flue tile cut to various lengths and stood on end. Such bottomless containers work fine if they are set on the ground; there, potting soil won't wash out through the bottom. You can buy concrete containers in many sizes and shapes from roadside molders of garden accessories, from whom you can also buy concrete benches and tables to use as stands to elevate your containers. Or you can hollow out driftwood and give it drainage holes so you can grow herbs, or chop cavities into the tops of stumps to accommodate potting soil and herb plants. But of all the styles of containers, two look best: those chiseled from stone or porous volcanic rock, and those cast from a mixture of mortar, peat moss, and Perlite and given a rough-hewn finish. These materials carry out the image of herbs as ancient plants that might long ago have thrived in such rock-girt environments. Plastic containers are probably the least suitable for growing herbs. It's not just that they can look tacky; more important, they don't evaporate water as the other materials do, so the soil in them stays wet longer. This can prove troublesome during prolonged wet weather.

Dealers list containers by their capacity in gallons. The diameter of the container as measured across the rim is not always a reliable guide to capacity, because the diameter-to-depth ratio can vary. Here's how one supplier of containers compares the capacity to the top diameter of "standard" containers, neither tall and skinny nor short and squat:

1 gallon = 7¼ inches
3 gallon = 10½ inches
5 gallon = 11¾ inches
7 gallon = 14 inches
10 gallon = 17¾ inches

Whiskey barrels sawed in half hold about thirty gallons, as do plastic garbage cans, the large ones that stand about two and a half feet high and measure two feet across the rim. As a rule of thumb, containers of one-gallon to three-gallon capacity work best for individual herb plants. Containers of five- to seven-gallon capacity are needed for three or more plants of the smaller herb species. In the South and West, where herbs such as sweet basil and lemon verbena grow large and shrubby, one or two plants can fill a thirty-gallon container by the end of the season.

I like to grow herbs in terra-cotta basins, big basins of five- to ten-gallon size, twenty to thirty inches rim to rim. These have more soil surface than tall containers and can accommodate five or more plants of small to medium size at maturity. Shallow basins or tubs hold more water in reserve than tall, slender containers of the same volume, an important consideration for working couples who can't be home to water plants on demand. You can make a lovely landscape in a large terra-cotta basin, complete with decorative stones, driftwood, miniature shrubs such as dwarf myrtle and boxwood, and herbs of various foliage and blossom colors. These basins, and terra-cotta pots, can be destroyed by freezing and thawing, though; come winter, I empty mine and store them indoors.

If you like the looks of terra-cotta strawberry jars, choose the larger sizes, eighteen to twenty-four inches high. Smaller jars dry out too fast. Plant your strawberry jars with small, low-growing, non-invasive herbs. Big plants such as anise hyssop, dill, and fennel soon grow out of scale with all but the very largest strawberry jars, and fast-spreading plants such as the mints soon become potbound. In general, the container should be one half to one third the size of the herb plant at maturity. Early in the growing season your container may look too large for the plant or plants in it, but with every week of good growing weather, your skill as a matchmaker will become more evident. If your herb plants prove too large for their containers, they will let you know by wilting severely in the afternoon sun, and they will tend to blow over in strong breezes.

Several herbs trail attractively and are ideal for hanging baskets and for half-baskets, which fit flat against walls or fences. Wire baskets lined with long-fiber sphagnum moss or koir (coconut fiber) are stronger than plastic baskets, an important consideration where wind can toss or twist them and break them loose from their hangers. One experience with small hanging baskets, which dry out quickly, will convince you to buy larger sizes; diameters of sixteen to twenty inches represent a good compromise between optimum rootball size and easily lifted weight.

Herbs for hanging baskets include both trailing types and compact, mounded varieties for planting in the center. Some of the best trailing types are the creeping thymes, common oregano, Cuban oregano, peppermint or spearmint, pennyroyal, creeping rosemary, false licorice (*Helichrysum petiolatum*), mignonette, and creeping germander. Dwarf sage, dwarf winter savory, the bush basils, and English thyme make neat mounds when young.

Landscaping with Containers of Herbs

A single large container planted with a mixture of herbs can be a landscape in itself. Plant trailing kinds around the rim, then work in toward the center with mounded forms. Set a single tall herb plant in the center, and you will have a container that will look good from all sides. For the most natural effect, use twice as many green plants as purple, gray, silver, or variegated ones.

Gardens made of several containers make the most impact in a landscape, especially when the containers are set at various levels, elevated on benches, tables, boxes, plant stands, cement blocks, or large inverted pots. Some gardeners order or build stair-stepped stands for containers, the favored arrangement for a kitchen garden. Seven containers of three- to five-gallon sizes, for example, can hold fifteen to twenty kinds of tea, salad, and savory herbs in an area no larger than a desktop, and at a convenient height.

Herbs like the larger terra-cotta strawberry jars. Silver-edged thyme and oregano are just getting started in this one.

Annual herbs that mature at a height of less than two feet are the easiest to work with. They grow much faster than the perennials and biennials, and you don't have to worry about overwintering them. You can grow tall herbs in large containers, but they'll fall over or break apart if you don't prune them. Among the most beau-

This scrumptious assortment of herbs and salad vegetables includes basil, parsley, romaine lettuce, oregano, peppers, English lavender, alpine strawberries, tarragon, and sweet marjoram.

tiful herbs for containers are 'African Blue' basil, 'Bergartten' sage, tricolor society garlic, and the variegated scented geraniums.

Many kinds of herbs are slow to hit their stride and don't really sprint until summer. You can spice up your containers with small plants of annual flowers, chosen for delicate blossoms and ferny foliage. Mix them with herbs as you plant new containers, or trim back perennial herbs and plug annual flowers into the open spaces. Look at the annuals as temporary; the herbs may push them out as the season progresses. My favorite flowers for mixing with herbs are the recently introduced white *Nierembergia* 'Mont Blanc', sweet alyssum, baby's breath, Swan River daisy, English daisy, baby-blue-eyes (*Nemophila*), lobelia, dianthus, Johnny-jump-up, and for early color, dwarf primula.

A finishing touch often overlooked on containers of herbs is a mulch of pebbles, crushed stone, or volcanic tufa, perhaps combined with larger decorative stones embedded in the surface of the soil. Mulches eliminate the problem of soil splashing on the foliage or floating away during heavy rains. They decrease water loss due to surface evaporation, and they look good. Decorative stones should be in scale with the size of the container and in keeping with its color and texture. Creeping herbs that spread over the rocky mulch and encircle embedded stones look especially good.

Soils for Containers

Garden soils are too dense to use in containers, and they tend to shrink away from the sides when dry. Instead, use either ready-made potting mixes (artificial soils) or mix your own. Ready-made potting soils are quite variable in porosity and weight, and their labels aren't very helpful in evaluating their quality. Look for a "professional" mix made of composted, pulverized pine or fir bark, high-quality peat moss, and perhaps a bit of Perlite. Avoid heavy mixtures that contain sand or a lot of water to increase their weight and make them appear to be good bargains. Appearances can be deceiving; very black mixtures are not necessarily the best.

Ready-made mixes contain a bit of limestone and just enough fertilizer to get plants off to a good start. Some contain 5 to 10 percent pasteurized soil, which helps feed plants and build up the population of beneficial soil organisms. Regardless of the ingredients, you should add pelleted dolomitic limestone to any artificial soil if you intend to use it to grow herbs. Mix in one quarter cup of pelleted limestone per gallon of potting soil. Do not add any fertilizer; wait until transplants have become adjusted to feed them.

If you make up your own artificial mix for growing herbs in containers, use two parts of pulverized pine or fir bark to one part of moistened Canadian sphagnum peat moss, and mix in pelleted limestone as described above. If you have any sifted compost, you can add a cup or two to each gallon of mixture, but expect some weeds to sprout, since a few seeds will have survived the heat of composting. Don't add sand unless you live in a very windy area and need the weight to help keep containers from blowing over.

Feeding and Watering

Organic plant foods are the choice of growers who believe that the type of fertilizer — chemical or organic — can affect the flavor and performance of herbs. These foods come in meal form or in liquid concentrates that you dilute in water and pour on the soil. Dry granular organic plant foods — soybean or cottonseed meal, for example — should be mixed into the soil so microorganisms can decompose them to make their nutrients fully available to plant roots.

Soluble chemical fertilizers come in liquid or crystalline forms. The crystalline forms are more expensive per unit of weight, but are so concentrated that after dilution they can actually be more economical. I have used several widely varying N-P-K analyses, from 20-20-20 through 15-30-15, and have not seen any difference in results in my container-grown herbs. My best results come from using organic fertilizers at half the recommended rate, in conjunction with liquid feeding at half rate.

Don't feed dry chemical fertilizers to plants in containers, as they

False licorice, *Helichrysum petiolatum,* a gray-leaved plant, is rapidly gaining favor for hanging baskets and half-baskets, as in this beauty.

A concrete bench makes a novel "container" for herbs. Thyme grows in pockets of potting soil in a thick layer of sphagnum moss. Twice-daily sprinkling with water is essential.

can burn the roots that grow near the surface of the soil. High-analysis nitrogen fertilizers such as urea and ammonium nitrate are especially dangerous to use on container plants.

You will need to feed herbs in containers much more often than herbs in the ground, because the frequent watering required by containers carries off plant nutrients. Long experience has shown that you should apply enough water each time for some excess to pour out of the drainage hole. This decreases the chance of fertilizer salts accumulating in the soil and injuring plant roots.

Herbs in containers need watering daily during warm weather, and twice daily when hot winds blow. If you can't be home for frequent watering, set your container inside a larger pot and stuff long-fiber sphagnum moss beneath and around it. Keep the moss moist; it will supply moisture while insulating the container from heat. If you have a number of herb containers, you may wish to invest in a drip irrigation system made of small-diameter "spaghetti tubes," with a separate emitter for each container. Such a system can be equipped with a timer so it will water your plants while you are away on vacation.

Absorbents and Surfactants

Absorbents are nontoxic polymers that resemble clear gelatin, and are marketed under a number of brand names. They hold more water than potting soils, and when mixed with them can increase the time between waterings. To obtain the best results, use them in hanging baskets, which dry out faster than freestanding containers. Mix them in, apply plain water, and let it soak in for an hour before applying liquid fertilizer for the first time.

Surfactants make water wetter, much as mild dishpan detergents do. They are useful for wetting the top layer of potting soils, which can become stubbornly dry during summer months, and for wetting kiln-dried, long-fiber sphagnum moss and dry, hard spots in your herb garden. Horticultural-grade surfactants have been tested for safety to plants; dishpan detergents have not.

These overgrown kitchen herbs share a weathered wood planter box. They need shearing and a shot of plant food.

Rhubarb, oregano, sage, lavender, and lemon balm share a planter box made of redwood.

Nutrient Deficiencies

In arid areas of the Southwest and West, container plants, especially citruses and broad-leaved evergreen herbs such as bay and myrtle, frequently show signs of iron chlorosis. Leaves appear to be thinner than usual, and light-colored tissue shows between darker green veins, especially on new growth. In extreme cases, the foliage turns pale yellow. This condition is caused by a number of factors, especially by alkaline soils in which salts accumulate, a condition most often seen during summer months. There is no perfect cure, but you can lessen the symptoms by feeding the affected plants with chelated iron, a slow-release form of this micronutrient. Increasing the frequency of watering can also help, by dissolving and leaching away some of the salts. Often iron deficiencies are accompanied by shortages of other micronutrients, such as magnesium, manganese, and zinc. Local garden supply dealers are usually aware of such conditions and carry corrective micronutrient blends.

Overwintering Herbs in Containers

In hardiness zone 8 and south, no special care is required to overwinter herbs in containers. Winters in zone 7 can be treacherous for half-hardy perennials such as creeping rosemary, fringed lavender, lemon grass, lemon verbena, and bay. In zone 7 and north, set containers of hardy herbs on the ground and draw soil or pinestraw around them to prevent the rootballs from freezing.

Where below-zero winter temperatures are common, you can employ a number of tactics to protect herbs from winter damage. The most effective defense is to slip the plants out of their containers, set them in a well-drained spot in the garden, and mulch them after the ground has begun to freeze. Placing containerized herbs in cold frames and mulching around them is nearly as effective. Gardeners have had some success with putting containers inside larger containers and filling the space between them with a two-inch layer of insulation such as Perlite. As an extra precaution, select herbs that

Colorful herbs look wonderful in ceramic and terra-cotta containers. On this patio, tricolor sage, golden sage, golden thyme, and parsley hold their own against bright geraniums and sweet alyssum.

Herbs, alpines, bonsai, and succulents cap a brick wall and a stone-mulched terrace supporting a greenhouse — a smart use of idle space.

are hardy in the next zone north of your location. If you garden in zone 6, for example, select herbs that are hardy through zone 5.

Like all plants grown in containers, herbs can die from desiccation in the winter. If you live in snowy country, remember to mound snow around and over the soil of containerized plants, not only to insulate them but to supply water as the snow gradually melts. Further south, if you have stored your water hoses for the winter, draw a bucket of tepid water and give your herbs a drink every week or so during dry weather.

Repotting Herbs

Certain herbs, such as the thymes, oreganos, and calamints, can survive for years in containers. Eventually, however, their roots begin to fill much of the area once occupied by soil. At that point, the plants become potbound and will no longer respond to feeding. If they could talk, they would tell you to take them out of the container, shake off the soil, straighten the roots, cut off those that are matted or that encircle the rootball, and pot them in the next larger size of container, filling beneath and around them with new potting soil. If you suspect that your plants are potbound, run a long knife around each rootball to free it from the container, turn it on its side, and

Setting containers on inverted pots, lengths of drainage tile, benches, and boxes makes the plants easier to water and groom.

slide the plant out. If the root system doesn't look congested, put the plant back in the container with as little disturbance as possible.

Potting soil used to grow herbs should not be reused. The best idea is to dump it on flower beds as a mulch. Used potting soils may look as good as new, but their nutrients are out of balance; salts may have accumulated, much of the fine fraction of particles will have disappeared, and root-rot organisms may be proliferating. In the first year of use, the natural decomposition of pine bark can release compounds that inhibit the growth of harmful soil organisms, but that activity slows appreciably in following years. In short, you are better off starting with new artificial soil every year.

Chapter 8

The Basics of Herb Gardening

Herbs are no harder to grow than ordinary flowers or vegetables, but the key to growing them superbly is thorough soil preparation and a continuing program of soil improvement tailored to your soil type.

Most garden soils fall into one of four broad categories. Heavy, dense, slow-draining clay soils predominate throughout the country. They can be reddish, gray, or yellow in color, or blackish if they have been under sod for several years. Clay soils are sticky when wet and hard as a brick when dry, and are composed of tiny laminar particles that can hold lots of water and plant nutrients. Despite their

This raised bed for a beginner is constructed of eight-foot-long four-by-fours filled with high-grade potting soil. It holds a birdbath as well as easy-to-grow herbs and edible flowers.

physical disadvantages, they can be transformed into easy-to-handle, productive soils for herb gardens.

At the other end of the spectrum, sandy soils are composed of relatively coarse, fast-draining particles that have little capacity to retain plant nutrients or water; consequently, they tend to be poor and dry. Sandy soils are generally light in color, but a high percentage of organic matter can darken them.

A third type, silty soil, is not too common, because it is found mostly in areas once covered by rivers or inundated by ancient lakes. Silty soils are composed of very fine particles that look like sand, but unlike sand they tend to pack down and become very hard when dry. Silty soils are typically light brown or yellow and are infertile.

The fourth type, loamy soil, is a mixture of the other three soils. Loams are usually dark in color, productive, easy to work, and retentive of moisture and plant nutrients. Physically, they can range from rather heavy clay loams to rather loose sandy loams. Herbs grow better in sandy loam than any other soil; therefore, this is the ideal soil, the one you should work toward.

Starting herbs indoors from seeds and cuttings is fascinating for children and adults alike. Eggs pierced for drainage, six-packs, and individual pots make good containers for sterile seed-starting mixtures.

An important step in growing herbs from seeds indoors is transplanting seedlings to individual pots. These seedlings are beginning to stretch a bit; they need transplanting, a cooler temperature, and more intense light.

Easily worked, naturally fertile sandy loams are occasionally found in nature but seldom around newly constructed homes, where the original topsoil has often been either hauled away and sold or buried beneath the infertile subsoil excavated during construction. Faced with such awful soil, most gardeners jump to the conclusion that hauling in topsoil is the only recourse. Actually, you are better off buying and mixing amendments into your soil to attain the desirable crumbly texture. Hauling in topsoil should be a last resort; stripping it from elsewhere is environmentally destructive, and it may also contain seeds of noxious weeds.

The goal in amending your soil is to achieve good aeration and its byproduct, good drainage; a pH level of 6.0 to 7.5; and the crumbly texture that makes soil easy to work. The organisms in this kind of soil can work at full speed to convert minerals and organic matter to nutrients that plant roots can assimilate.

Improving Clay Soils

Clay or clay loams tend to remain wet and cold in the spring, but once dry are slow to absorb water. It is hard to find a time when you can work clay soil without having it wad up into sticky clods or fracture into dust. Although gardeners regard clay soils as a cross they have to bear, in actuality these soils have positive qualities that sandy soil does not. Their exceedingly fine particles are electrochemically active and can attract and hold plant nutrient ions in reserve, which results in efficient utilization of fertilizer. Also, clay soils hold considerably more water than sands, which evens out the wet-dry cycles between rains and irrigations.

You can improve the stubbornest heavy clay soil by opening it up with amendments, which modify the soil structure and texture. Sand and organic matter are the two most commonly used amendments; these are bulky materials that help granulate the soil. Granular soil has lots of pore space between particles, and the openings allow essential oxygen to penetrate the soil to a depth of several inches. The pore space in granular soils enables water to soak into the surface rather than run off, and to percolate down to lower layers of the soil, where it is held in reserve.

Sand is the least expensive amendment for loosening clay soil, but if you don't want concrete, you must use it in conjunction with organic matter. Not all sands are alike. Builder's sand, also called sharp sand, works better than river sand because its particles have sharp edges, whereas river sand particles have been tumbled and smoothed. Chicken grit from a feed-and-seed store works even better than sand, but is more expensive. If you live near a granite quarry, you can get the best granulator of all, granite meal or granite dust.

"Organic matter" describes a multitude of materials, some good for the soil, some bad. Two of the most popular are sphagnum peat moss and sawmill byproducts, such as pulverized pine or fir bark and composted sawdust. Pasteurized, packaged cattle manure can be substituted for about one quarter of the total organic matter needed, but it contains too much ammonia to be used as the sole source. Compost made from yard wastes is excellent but is seldom available in sufficient quantities to make much of an impact on soil structure. Leaves are good but are too coarse to mix with the soil unless they have been shredded or composted. Raw sawdust should also be composted, as it can stunt growth and cause plants to turn yellow if mixed directly into the soil. Chipped wood is too coarse and resistant to decay to be used for soil improvement, but it makes a good mulch. Raw manure and stable litter are usually full of weed seeds and bring in more problems than they cure.

Something wonderful happens when you mix generous amounts of sharp sand and organic matter into clay soil. They work together to open the soil and set the stage for granulation. In the presence of the abundant oxygen that enters the loosened soil, beneficial organisms work to "glue" large and small soil particles into bunches like grapes, further increasing pore space. In the process, they also convert minerals into forms that plant roots can absorb.

Here's a sure-fire method of getting the right compromise among aeration, drainage, and the retention of desirable amounts of water and plant nutrients. Start with moderately dry clay soil, not wet enough to be plastic nor dry enough to approach the hardness of a brick. Dig it to a depth of six to nine inches and break up the clods. Remove the debris, stones, and clumps of grass and weeds, and roughly level the soil with a rake. Spread a two-inch layer of organic matter on top, and over it a two-inch layer of builder's sand, chicken grit, or granite meal. Mix them thoroughly throughout the dug soil, being careful not to leave pockets of sand or organic matter. After modification, your clay soil should be neither loose nor dense but moderately fast-draining, with the ability to retain good supplies of moisture and plant nutrients.

Throughout the East and Southeast, new gardens generally need lime. However, liming is not required for soils where the climate is arid, nor for soils underlain by limestone. Your local nursery will know if soils in your neighborhood need lime to grow good flowers, vegetables, and herbs, and how much to apply. Ask for pelleted dolomitic lime, which releases calcium and magnesium ions considerably faster than ground agricultural limestone.

Raised Beds

Rather than go to the work of amending their clay soil, some gardeners opt to build raised beds on top of it. They build frames, set them level on tilled soil, pin them in place with stakes driven into

the ground, and fill the frames with potting soil made with equal parts of pulverized pine or fir bark and sphagnum peat moss, and perhaps pasteurized cattle manure and homemade compost. In this way, raised beds provide an ideal soil, and they also eliminate soil compaction because of foot traffic. However, many gardeners omit an important step, that of spading deeply enough to bring up a bit of native soil to mix with the potting soil — 10 to 20 percent by volume. This breaks the moisture transmission barrier that might otherwise form at the interface between the potting soil and the underlying clay.

Improving Sandy Soil

Gardeners who have to deal with sticky clay soil envy people who garden on sand. It is certainly a lot easier to work with, but sand has its drawbacks: it dries out rapidly, gets very hot in the summer, and has virtually no capacity to retain water, plant nutrients, or lime. So how do you make sand more hospitable to plants? Not by adding clay; its particles are extremely fine and will literally slip through the sand and lodge in dense layers of hardpan a foot or two down in the soil. Hardpans interfere with the drainage of water by gravity and with its upward movement through capillary action.

The way to improve the water and nutrient storage capacity of sand is to mix organic matter with it as you prepare the bed. But organic matter also tends to slip through sand particles and escape to lower levels, and it oxidizes rather rapidly in hot sand, so you need to add more at least every other year. It is difficult to add organic matter to beds planted densely with perennial herbs. About the best you can do is to mix generous amounts into the planting holes when you replace or divide herbs, and cover any exposed soil with mulch. In northern climates, where perennial herbs are dormant for five to six months and die back nearly to the ground, you can spread a light topping of organic mulch over the entire garden each fall, no deeper than half an inch.

Sands that develop from the weathering of sandstone or granite are generally acidic and require yearly applications of pelleted lime

Prick out individual seedlings with a pencil point to preserve as much of the root system as possible. Transplant the seedlings to the same depth as they were in the seed pot.

Herbs will grow for a while in small pots, which can be arranged in baskets or other ornamental containers. Soon, however, plants such as these basils will outgrow their little containers.

105

to maintain a pH level of 6.0 to 7.5, the optimum range for herbs. Other sands are derived from ancient seabed deposits and are calcareous; that is, they are naturally high in calcium and perhaps magnesium and don't need lime. You need to know the approximate pH of your soil, because adding lime to a calcareous soil can raise the pH so high that vital micronutrients are locked up in insoluble compounds. Either have your soil tested by the Cooperative Extension Service or ask your neighborhood nurseryman if lime is needed locally on sandy soil.

Improving soil is an ongoing process, because organic matter decomposes under the action of soil organisms. The organic fraction of soils is dynamic and declines under cultivation. Decomposition occurs faster in warm climates. You will need to add organic matter at least every other year.

Another approach is to plant your herbs rather far apart and mulch between them. You can walk on the mulch without compacting the soil, and earthworms will carry organic matter deep into the soil as the mulch decomposes. Be careful not to mulch deeply over the crowns of perennial herbs, however, as the mulch can hold moisture and cause the herbs to die during extended wet weather.

Sun and Shade

Most herbs prefer full sun, except in zones 7 through 10, where afternoon shade helps to reduce the stress on plants. Over the balance of North America, how well herbs grow is directly proportional to the duration and intensity of sunlight. The more direct sunlight they get, the better sun-loving herbs will thrive. But you can grow herbs pretty well where they get half a day of full sun plus reflected sunlight at other times. Sunlight bounces off the ground as well as buildings and walls, especially from mid-morning through mid-afternoon, and can supplement the photosynthetic activity generated by sunlight falling directly on leaves.

If you have doubts whether a given site will receive enough sunlight to grow herbs, wait until midsummer to make the determination. During spring and fall months, shadows are long, and you might erroneously conclude that your chosen site is too shady. In midsummer, the path of the sun is high in the sky, and shaded areas are smaller. You will know your herbs are not receiving enough sunlight if they stretch and become leggy.

Shade comes in various degrees. Light shade is cast by trees with open canopies of foliage, latticework trellises, or ferny vines on fences. Moderate shade is cast by limbed-up trees that allow a lot of reflected light to fall on plants growing nearby. Heavy shade is cast by low-branching trees with dense canopies and by buildings, solid fences, walls, and hills.

Although many herbs grow fairly well in light shade, only a few can tolerate moderate shade, and none can endure dense shade. Many of the herbs with broad leaves or with a dense canopy of foliage, such as lady's mantle, French sorrel, arugula, and parsley, tolerate light shade fairly well. Sweet woodruff not only tolerates shade but actually grows better in light to moderate shade.

Herb gardeners in Florida, along the Gulf Coast, and at low elevations in the West have found that many herbs that require full sun in the North prefer light shade all day long, or shade in the afternoon, in their area. This may be because light shade reduces stress on the plants, but it may also be partly because of reduced damage from nematodes, which are worse in hot, dry soils that receive no shade.

Feeding and Watering

Herb literature is full of advice to grow herbs "lean," in rather poor, dry soil. Although most herbs are descended from wild plants whose native habitat is dry and rocky, they will grow better with a moderate level of plant food and an occasional deep watering. Feeding and watering can be overdone, though — too much nitrogen, for example, will cause sweet basil to develop an odd flavor.

Don't hesitate to feed your herbs lightly two or three times during the growing season, but discontinue feeding at least a month before the average date of the first fall frost. Feeding herbs too late in the fall can "tenderize" the perennials and cause them to succumb to winter's cold. If you are an organic gardener, don't broadcast dry organic plant foods such as soybean or cottonseed meal, tankage, or blood meal; for herbs to utilize these nutrients best, you need to dig them in around the plants, which isn't practical with spreading or creeping plants such as thyme and mint. A better option is to use liquid organic fertilizers made from fish byproducts, which you can pour around plants or spray on the foliage when the sun is not intense. Some gardeners fill the nutrient needs of their herbs by dressing enriched compost between plants; they fortify garden compost with chicken, sheep, or rabbit manure and let it heat to kill weed seeds before applying it. These manures are much richer in plant nutrients than cattle or horse manure.

In our greenhouses we used a combination of soluble crystalline fertilizers and controlled-release fertilizers to feed herbs, but we found that an occasional feeding with organic plant food improved the appearance and production of cut herbs. Evidently organic fertilizers have something in them that manufactured plant foods lack. We made "manure tea" and poured it on the soil of container plants, a method that eliminated potential problems with weed seeds in the manure. To make manure tea, put five pounds of rabbit, chicken, or sheep manure in a cloth bag and hang it over the edge of a thirty-gallon plastic garbage can filled with water. Every day or so, swirl the bag around in the water. When the manure tea has begun to smell, but not enough to offend your neighbors, pour it around the plants. Dump the leached manure into your compost heap, where any weed seeds in it will be killed by the heat of composting.

If your soil drains well, it will pay you to install a drip irrigation system and water once or twice weekly during hot, dry spells. We had three acres of herbs under drip irrigation, and they thrived. I let each section of the irrigation system run for at least an hour. To check the depth of penetration, I dug down beside an emitter; I found that an hour of watering moistened my sandy loam more than a foot deep. Drip irrigation does not wet the plants' foliage, which sets up favorable conditions for disease spores to germinate, and it saves on the water bill. We experimented with various kinds of

Six weeks after being transplanted to individual cells in a six-pack, these young plants of sweet marjoram are well grown. They will adapt to their new environment better if the matted roots are loosened before planting.

tubing and concluded that "leaky hose" was the most durable and efficient.

Feeding and watering herbs in containers is a whole different ballgame; see Chapter 7.

Mulching

Mulches suppress weeds, conserve water, reduce erosion and soil splash, and (to me) are more attractive than bare ground. They can

Flagstones turned on edge frame a raised bed planted with purple basil, tricolor sage, lady's mantle, scented geraniums, and, as an edging, gray santolina.

be either organic, such as pine, fir, or hardwood bark, saltmarsh hay, pine needles, or shredded, partly composted leaves, or mineral, such as cracked pea gravel, pebbles, or volcanic tufa.

Herb gardeners in hardiness zones 3 through 5 seldom use organic mulches on slow-draining clay soils, as they tend to keep the soil too cool and hold in so much moisture that the crowns of perennial herbs can rot. In cool climates, it is better to use mulches of coarse sand, crushed pea gravel, pebbles, or tufa, which absorb solar heat during the day and radiate it at night. They also inhibit foliage diseases by reducing soil splash and by drying off so rapidly that disease organisms can't incubate in them. These mineral mulches present three problems, however. They are difficult to rake free of leaves (it can be done, but not easily); they make a good seedbed for weed and tree seeds; and you have to be careful not to mix them with the soil when planting or replacing herbs. To reduce the weed problem in a new herb bed, lay down spun-bonded landscape cloth and spread the mulch over it. Cut holes through the cloth to set out plants.

Organic mulches are plentiful and inexpensive in zones 6 through 10, and work well around herbs if they are not pulled up close to the crowns of plants. On Savory Farm we mulched our herbs with three inches of hardwood sawdust but were careful to scatter a generous application of organic fertilizer before mulching. The fertilizer prevented nitrogen drawdown, which results when soil organisms draw nitrogen from the soil in order to break down the sawdust. We had to apply a fresh two-inch layer of mulch yearly, but I didn't mind the labor of hauling and spreading it. It reduced weeding from a constant chore to an occasional light job, and helped keep our herbs growing strongly during periods of drought.

My favorite mulch is ground hardwood bark, a sawmill byproduct. It mats down and doesn't wash away during thunderstorms. It doesn't last quite as long as pulverized pine bark mulch, but it weathers to a nice grayish brown that looks good with herbs. It doesn't cause nitrogen drawdown except on very poor soils, and a light application of fertilizer can rectify that. If you happen to mix a bit of organic mulch into the soil while planting or dividing herbs, it should help the plants to catch and grow better.

Herb Pests

I wish I could tell you that your herb garden will always be free of insect pests and diseases, but it isn't true. While northern herb gardens may have negligible damage from insects and plant diseases, the number and variety of problems increase in gardens where the climate is milder and more humid. Herbs are attacked by fewer pests than most other garden plants, possibly because their strong aromas evolved to make them less attractive to insects and grazing animals. But they are not without pests, and you need either to prevent or to control those pests with the same methods you would use for vegetable crops.

On Savory Farm, we had insect and disease infestations that were more severe than those in home gardens, because the large patches of herbs of different kinds tended to draw more pests than a plant or two of a given species would. We shipped cut herbs to restaurants, so we had to produce plants that were without blemishes. Now that my herbs are concentrated in a garden of about two hundred square feet, my tolerance for blemishes has risen considerably, and also, I don't see nearly as many insects and diseases as I did in our three acres of commercial herbs. Perhaps it is because my garden is bordered by a sizable meadow of native wildflowers, which supports a great number and variety of predatory insects and wild birds.

On our herb farm, several species of leafhoppers were the most troublesome insects, with spider mites second and harlequin bugs third. We had virtually no problem with aphids, thanks to a population of hungry predatory ladybugs and lacewing flies. Praying mantids helped a bit, but we never had many of them, perhaps because the many insectivorous birds on the place gobbled them up along with the pestiferous insects. We did have a large population of predatory rove beetles, which helped to control insect pests.

Starting from Seeds

Most herb gardeners prefer to buy started plants; they never start from seeds. That's too bad; some kinds of herbs grow quickly and easily from direct seeding in the garden. Many of these don't transplant well, and never perform as well when grown from started plants. We always direct-seeded alexanders and angelica in our garden as soon as the seeds were mature enough to shake from the heads, and virtually every seed sprouted. Seeds of these two species drop off in germination rates rapidly as they age, so you may wish to buy a mother plant or two to grow your own seeds for direct seeding.

We direct-seeded anise, anise hyssop, anise-scented marigold, arugula, borage, caraway, chamomile, cilantro, upland cress, dill, epazote, fennel, mache or corn salad, safflower, sesame, and sorrel. After we learned that arugula, chervil, chamomile, cilantro, dill, and fennel self-sowed generously, we left a few plants in each row to drop seeds for a succession crop of volunteer seedlings.

In addition, we sowed nasturtium and calendula seeds for edible flowers, and second and succeeding crops of sweet basil. (We started our early crop of basil indoors ten weeks before the frost-free date.) We thinned direct-seeded herbs when the plants were quite small and transplanted the surplus seedlings. To sow the herbs, I used a triangular Warren hoe to cut furrows about two inches deep in the prepared soil of raised beds. I scattered seeds thinly down the furrows but did not cover them; instead, I walked heel-to-toe down each furrow to press the seeds firmly into the soil. It worked like a charm.

Other kinds of herbs have tiny seeds that produce very small, slow-growing seedlings, which can be swamped by weeds, or their seeds germinate slowly and unevenly. Since some of these don't grow well from tip cuttings, they are usually started from seeds indoors under fluorescent lights or on a warm west- or south-facing windowsill. These include common strains (not named cultivars) of burnet, chervil, chives, comfrey, germander, hops, hyssop, lavender, lovage, sweet marjoram, oregano, parsley, peppers, rosemary, garden sage, salvia, common or French thyme, wormwood, and yarrow.

At the University of Minnesota Landscape Arboretum, two cultivars of the universally useful and beautiful creeping thymes flow around a glacier-smoothed boulder.

Stones look good among herbs, especially if they are embedded so that only about a third shows. These flat stones make steps on a steep slope planted with golden thyme and thrift at the U.S. Botanical Garden, in Washington, D.C.

Two of the most difficult herbs to grow from seeds are rosemary and lavender. The seeds germinate rather poorly and over a period of several weeks. Once you have mother plants of lavender and rosemary, you can propagate more from tip cuttings from midsummer on.

Starting from Cuttings or Divisions

Certain herbs are always grown from tip cuttings or root cuttings, as they either don't form fertile seeds or don't come true to type when grown from seeds. These include all the mints, French tarragon, lemon verbena, the hardy rosemarys, and the tender lavenders. In addition, any named cultivar of any species must be propagated vegetatively in order to have it look and perform just like its mother plant.

Once you have plants of herbs growing in your garden, you can reproduce them by dividing their crowns. Herbs with single, central stems can't be divided in this fashion: sweet basil, anise hyssop, and most of the salvias, for example. However, the mints, thymes, calamints, saturejas or savories, catmints, bergamots, and mountain mints either have underground stems or root wherever a joint touches the ground, so they are quite easy to multiply by vegetative division.

Weeds

If you don't mulch your herbs, you will have to weed. That's the problem with bare soil; weeds grow in it, from either seeds or underground stolons. You can remove weeds by pulling or cultivate the soil to dry it out and kill the emerging seedlings. But if you dig too deep with hoes or tined cultivators, you will worsen the weed problem by bringing seeds from deep layers up to the surface. A much better technique is to use an implement that disturbs only the top half-inch of soil yet pulverizes it and kills most of the weed seedlings. My favorite tool for cultivating is an action hoe, which resembles a stirrup. Both the leading and trailing edges of the thin serrated blade are sharp, to cut weed roots as you push and pull. A Dutch hoe is similar, and a small hand tool, the Cape Cod weeder, also cultivates to a shallow depth.

However you cultivate your herbs, don't allow broad-leaved weeds or grasses to grow large before you remove them. Larger weeds have to be pulled out, and you will often uproot herb plants in the process. If weeds or clumps of grass get away from you and grow large, try digging their roots out with a dandelion digger, a hand tool that has a long, slender iron shaft with the digging end flattened so you can pry taproots out of the ground. You may have to remove large plants of deep-rooted perennial weeds such as dandelions and curly dock with a spade in order to get all of the root. If you leave a piece of the taproot behind, it will sprout and send up a new top.

Growing Herbs Indoors

If you like to season your summer meals with fresh herbs, just imagine harvesting sprigs of fresh home-grown herbs during the winter. It's not impossible, but unless you live in the South or West, you will need to supplement the sun with fluorescent tubes or halide lamps and modify the dry air around your plants.

In the North, insufficient light is the major problem of growing plants indoors, but bone-dry, heated air during the winter runs a close second. From Halloween through late March, the days are so short and the skies are so often overcast that plants can't replace lost food reserves and gradually starve. The thin foliage of herbs can't keep up with the transpiration rate caused by superdry, furnace-heated air. Tender new foliage and the margins of older leaves turn dry and look scorched. Pouring on water only compounds the problem, for unless a plant is actively growing, it can't use much water.

Across the South and West, winters are shorter, and winter days are longer and brighter. Yet the sunlight indoors during the dead of winter, even under the most favorable conditions, will not meet the full solar energy requirements of the most important species of sun-loving herbs, such as basil.

The most popular indoor plant-growing lights are fluorescent tubes mounted under reflectors on movable carts or stationary plant stands. They work best when supplemented with an incandescent bulb or two. With fluorescent lights burning for fourteen to sixteen hours a day, you can keep annual herb plants such as basil, biennials such as parsley, and perennials such as spearmint producing sprigs for cutting all winter long. French tarragon, however, needs to be exposed to two months of cold weather to supply its requirement for a winter dormancy period. When you bring the chilled tarragon plants indoors and place them under lights, they will resume growing within two to three weeks.

The critical factor in growing plants under fluorescent lights is to place their tops at least two and not more than six inches from the tubes; use the lesser distance for seedlings, the greater for older plants with larger leaves. It is also critical to maintain a good level of humidity around your herbs. Either spritz them twice a day with a

An end-of-season array of pots on a windowsill hold ornamental cabbage, basil, geraniums, parsley, and hot peppers transplanted from the garden. They will last until the days grow short and dark.

hand-pump spray bottle or set them on a tray of pebbles sitting in a shallow layer of water.

When you grow herb plants under fluorescent lights, you need to "grow cool." Optimum temperatures for sizable plants are 65°F during the day and 60° at night. These temperatures are in keeping with the light levels from the fluorescent tubes, which can be compared to light to moderate shade outdoors. The latest models of full-spectrum fluorescent bulbs duplicate more than 90 percent of the spectrum of the sun, including red, to make the colors of blossoms and foliage appear true to life.

A stronger source of supplemental light is metal halide lamps, sold under such names as Super Lumen Output Bulbs. They look like big incandescent bulbs under square, vented reflectors. Such lamps have been used for many years for lighting expensive commercial crops during the winter; they cast more energy on a given area than fluorescent tubes. They work well, but they cost more to buy and to operate than fluorescent tubes, and they generate substantially more heat. Optimum growing temperatures with metal halide lamps are somewhat higher than with fluorescent tubes — 65° to 70° in the day, 60° to 65° at night — thanks to the higher intensity of light.

Another way to grow herbs indoors for kitchen use does not require supplementary lighting. Pot up established herb plants from the garden in the fall, well before the first frost, clean off insects with sprays of insecticidal soap, and place them on sunny windowsills. They will flourish for several weeks, until the days become too short and dreary to sustain growth. At that point, use them up and sacrifice the plants rather than try to carry them through the winter.

What if you merely wish to overwinter half-hardy herb plants indoors rather than grow them for cutting? Rosemary and bay are the only plants that are frequently overwintered in zone 6 and north. Some gardeners have good luck every winter with setting these plants near south- or west-facing windows, but not so near that radiated cold can injure them. Others routinely lose plants, and the reason is usually overwatering. If you have had difficulty overwintering rosemary, bay, and perhaps lavender, try watering them only once every two or three weeks.

 *Chapter 9*

Harvesting and Preserving Herbs

Harvesting herbs, whether for fresh, frozen, or dried use in cooking, for fashioning into wreaths or swags, for bottling in wine, vinegar, or oil, or for preserving in herb butters, pesto, and potpourris, is one of the most ancient and gratifying of human rituals. Just how you go about it depends in part on how you intend to use them. Take just the tips for fresh use or freezing; take twigs for drying whole for winter seasonings; and take long stems or branches for dried arrangements.

Nothing makes a house smell more like a home than bunches and swags of herbs hung to dry.

Harvesting Culinary Herbs

Culinary herbs are best when fresh, and next best when frozen. You can use them in salads and fruit dishes as well as in cooked preparations. I know a chef in Columbus, Ohio, the owner of a German restaurant, who won't use dried herbs. He insists on personally seasoning each serving of stir-fried fresh vegetables, his specialty, with a generous pinch of mixed chopped basil, parsley, oregano, and lemon thyme. To preserve the flavor and aroma, he adds the herbs to the vegetables after they are cooked. The heat from the sizzling vegetables is enough to release the aromatic oils in the herbs, and the delicious aroma wafts across the restaurant.

Frozen herbs taste much like the fresh product but lose their shape and texture in freezing. They should be used in cooked dishes or drinks where appearance doesn't matter. The bouquet and flavor of herbs also keep pretty well in wine, oil, vinegar, and butter. Dried herbs, no matter how carefully they are prepared, do not have the same flavor as fresh ones. Some, such as lemon balm, lose much of their taste; others develop strong, intense flavors that little resemble the fresh product and are best employed in cooked dishes.

When gathering fresh herbs for seasoning, harvest tender, vegetative tips of branches with four to six leaves, or two- to three-inch tips of fine-leaved kinds such as thyme. Avoid stems tipped with flowers; they will have lost flavor through the effort of flowering. When we harvested fresh herbs for shipping, we preferred to take them just after the morning dew had dried. When we attempted to harvest in the midday or afternoon heat, the herbs wilted before we could get them out of the field. Another window for harvesting was dusk, after the plants had recovered their crispness but while we still had enough light to see clearly.

At Savory Farm, we pioneered in post-harvest conditioning of herbs so that they would keep for a week to ten days under refrigeration. Storage isn't an imperative for home herb growers, but it is convenient, and having fresh herbs handy in the refrigerator encourages you to use them in new ways. We never washed herbs from our fields, but packed them loosely in perforated plastic bags. We placed

This gardener pinches the flowers off her sweet basil to encourage the plants to produce more leaves for fresh use. She will freeze her basil crop before it is killed by fall frost.

the bags, with the tops open, in a refrigerator at 41°F. In an hour or two, depending on the dryness of the foliage, we closed each bag with a twist fastener. The perforations prevented condensation and subsequent decay, yet didn't allow the herbs to dry out significantly. You can make your own perforated bag by using a paper punch to punch eight holes in a large, zip-closure freezer bag.

Preparing fresh herbs for kitchen use is easy, but it takes a bit of time to remove the leaves from some species. Large, leafy herbs such as basil and parsley are a breeze to prepare, but herbs such as thyme have woody stems, and their tiny leaflets have to be stripped off. If the herbs are to flavor a soup or stew, it's easier to make a bouquet garni instead. Combine sprigs of three or four kinds of fresh herbs, wrap them in cheesecloth, and hang the bouquet garni over the edge of the pot. The stronger herbs — rosemary, thyme, oregano, savory, and such — are used mostly for flavoring meats, poultry, cheeses, and bland vegetables. The more delicate or fruity-tasting herbs are used to flavor fish, salads, drinks, and fruit dishes. When you cook with herbs, remember to use twice as much of the fresh herbs as the dried product, except for fresh rosemary, which you use in equal quantities.

Herbal vinegars, wines, oils, pestos, and butters find many uses in cooking and make treasured gifts. To flavor liquids, insert in a bottle two or three sprigs of fresh, washed herbs that have been dried just enough to evaporate surface moisture, pour the liquid in, and stopper or cap the bottle tightly. Let it sit in a warm, dark area for a month before tasting. If the flavor seems weak, strain out the spent herbs and insert fresh twigs. Again, let the bottle sit for a month before removing the herbs. I like to use purple basil or purple garden sage in liquids; these herbs impart a rich pink color in addition to the desired flavor. Basil, sage, French tarragon, thyme, oregano, and dill are often used in wines, oils, and vinegars. Some people leave the herbs in the bottles in order to identify the contents, but they risk having the herbs spoil and ruin the liquid.

Herb butters and pestos are usually prepared at the end of the season, when frost threatens to nip the crop. Use clarified butter if you have the time to make it, and mix in finely chopped herbs, just enough to add a bit of color. Then if you use the butter as a spread for bread or toast, the herb flavor won't be overpowering. Freeze the herb butter and use it to get the natural flavor of herbs during the winter, when fresh herbs are either very expensive or unavailable. Check the condition of the frozen herb butter occasionally; sixty to ninety days is its usual life.

Make pesto with puréed fresh basil flavored with pine nuts and fresh garlic, virgin olive oil, and salt to taste. Test the taste and consistency when the pesto is still in the blender and modify it as desired. Chefs are experimenting with other herb and nut combinations for pesto: parsley with walnuts or pine nuts with rosemary or sage instead of basil, for example.

Many herb enthusiasts use the branch tips of attractive herbs such as cinnamon basil, spearmint, and peppermint as garnishes, or edible herb flowers such as chives, garlic chives, nasturtiums, and calendulas, whole or scattered over salads. It is always a good idea to soak

This wreath of dried herbs and everlastings by Carol Czechowski shows a good command of both drying and flower arranging techniques. Some of the materials were air-dried; others were dried with silica gel.

125

herbs or flowers in water for at least thirty minutes before drying them and using them as a garnish, to flush out insects that might be in hiding.

Harvesting Herbs for Crafts

One of the most pleasant tasks in herb gardening is gathering and drying sweetly fragrant or flowering herbs: lavender, lemon verbena, anise hyssop, anise-scented marigold, sage, scented pelargoniums, and such. Gathering flowering stems or leafy branches will change the appearance of your herb landscape, no doubt about it, but a thorough watering and feeding will bring new growth and a fresh face to cut-back plants. If you are gathering long branches to dry for kitchen use, wreaths, swags, and dry arrangements, you need not disfigure your landscape herbs; take every third branch instead of chopping back the entire plant. Mid-morning, just after the dew has dried, is the best time to harvest for maximum aroma.

Drying Herbs

Most gardeners air-dry herbs when they have a lot to process, and it works just fine if you dry the herbs in the dark with good ventilation. One comparison of the taste and color of herbs dried in the sun with those dried in the dark will convince you. Sun blackens basil and bleaches other herbs while changing and diminishing the flavor.

Old homes have dark attics or barns that work well for drying herbs. They provide warmth and darkness; all that is needed is ventilation to carry away moisture and an electric fan to move the air. The second best location is a utility room in an outbuilding where the temperature is uncomfortably warm during the summer. Basements are usually too humid for drying herbs, but spare rooms will do if you can darken them and ventilate them with a fan. Crack a door to allow moisture to escape. Total or near-total darkness works best.

Here's how to air-dry herbs. Tie small bunches together and hang them upside down. Set a fan far enough away so that the blast

You'll find a place for all your dried herb flowers and everlastings. Here, bunches of dried flowers discourage people from sitting on a fragile antique chair.

Arrangements of herb flowers and foliage are limited only by your imagination and by what happens to be blooming when you design them. This one, created at Gilberg's Perennial Farms, in Glencoe, Missouri, includes lavender, garlic chives, tansy, purple basil seed heads, sorrel, betony, and anise hyssop.

Instead of letting flower heads dry on the plants and shorten their bloom season, harvest them for arrangements or for making potpourri. These flowers include old roses, lavender, borage, marguerite, dill, and ornamental allium.

doesn't tangle the bunches; run it on a low setting. Some gardeners cover the herbs with open-ended hoods of newspapers to keep dust off during long storage. Basil is the most difficult of the herbs to dry without blackening, and the dried product is nothing like as good as fresh or frozen basil.

A gas stove with an oven is one of the best driers for herbs. Turn the oven on to the lowest setting, set the herbs inside on cookie tins, and crack the door to allow moisture to escape and to avoid over-heating and cooking the herbs. If you have a pilot light that keeps the oven slightly warm, it alone may dry herbs over a two- or three-day period. Electric ovens are often too hot, but my electric oven can be turned down to 110 degrees for slow drying of herbs. Fast drying won't work; either it will harden the outer surfaces while leaving the interior moist, or it will evaporate the volatile oils that give herbs their special aroma and flavor.

It is also possible to microwave herbs at low settings, but because microwave ovens can handle only relatively short pieces and not many of them, you can use them only for drying herb leaves or branch tips for kitchen or craft use. Remove the herbs every thirty minutes, turn them over, and give the pile a quarter turn to insure even drying throughout.

Dehydrators give the best results for small batches of short twigs or leaves of herbs. The combination of gentle heat and abundant air flow preserves high color and aroma. Follow the directions for drying herbs. Just remember, if you wash the herbs prior to drying, hang them to drain before attempting to dry them in an oven or dehydrator.

One of the most appreciated gifts for an herb crafter is a screen-covered tray for drying petals, leaves, and twigs of fine-leaved herbs such as thyme. The usual size is eighteen by twenty-four inches, but larger trays give you room to spread out the products for faster drying. The better trays have cross-struts beneath the screen to prevent sagging and a two-inch-high slat around the perimeter to prevent spilling. Well-built and well-finished drying trays are treasured and passed down in families. Set them on bricks in a darkened room, with a fan directed on them to speed up the process. Herb growers in dry climates can get by without fans, but they are necessary in humid climates to prevent molding. The entire house benefits from the delightful fragrance of herbs drying on frames.

Whichever method you use for drying herbs, remove them before they become so dry that they crumble when touched. Store your dried culinary herbs whole in large jars. Don't rub them until you

The makings of potpourri and salt substitutes — dried rose petals and herbs — can be stored in sealed jars in a cool basement.

are about to use them, in order to maintain their maximum potency. If the leaves are brittle-dry but some of the stems are still limber, be sure to put a few pouches of desiccants in each jar before sealing. You can recycle desiccants from bottles of pills or cans of coffee, or wrap two tablespoons of powdered milk in two thicknesses of facial tissue and secure the package with a rubber band. Store only one kind of herb per jar to prevent mingling of flavors and aromas.

Freezing Herbs

To freeze herbs, spread leaves one layer deep on a cookie tin and put it in the freezer. When they are frozen solid — and it doesn't take long — remove them and store them in a freezer bag. Basil is the herb most often frozen, and it frequently blackens instead of retaining its pretty green color. Don't be put off by the color; the black comes from enzymatic action, not from decay, and the good taste will still be there. Test a few leaves first; if they blacken, experiment with air-drying the basil in the refrigerator for half a day to remove some of the moisture before freezing. It is easy to chop parsley, dill, and chervil in a food processor and store them in the freezer, ready to use whenever you need them.

I have puréed herbs, mixed them with just enough water to make a paste, spooned them into ice cube trays, and frozen them. The cubes of frozen herbs can be popped out of the trays and stored in labeled freezer bags, then dropped into drinks, fruit dishes, or cooked foods a minute before serving. Freezing in ice cubes is an excellent way to preserve the fresh flavor and aroma of spearmint and peppermint and the delicate flavor of fresh dill and sweet fennel. One cube of frozen herb is equivalent to between one half and one tablespoon of fresh herb.

I urge you to use the herbs you grow. A twig of fresh tarragon laid on chicken and broiled, a sprig of fresh spearmint crushed and rubbed inside a tea glass, a bunch of dried lavender nestled between pillowcases in the linen closet — these can make a good life even better.

Dried flowers of perennials and herbs can be made into all kinds of decorations, as seen at Well-Sweep Herb Farm, in Port Murray, New Jersey.

Chapter 10

Herbs for Beautiful Landscapes

Most of the herbs in this chapter qualify for inclusion on several grounds, but the overriding criterion is their beauty and usefulness in garden settings. You won't find plain or awkward herbs here, except for a few that are essential to good cooking. The herbs are arranged alphabetically by species, abbreviated "spp."

Achillea spp.
Yarrow

Once valued for their medicinal properties, the yarrows are today more likely to be classified as flowering perennials than as herbs. These are

Two edible ornamentals share this border at Inniswood Metro Gardens, in Columbus, Ohio: garlic chives, just coming into flower, and the variegated nasturtium 'Alaska'.

135

quadruple-threat plants that give meaning to the word *everlasting*. They bloom over a long period, make long-lasting fresh cut flowers, last for years as dried flowers in most cases, and are hardy from zone 3 to 9.

The most popular yarrows for the garden and for drying are the gray-leaved, yellow- or gold-flowered *Achillea* 'Moonshine' and *A.* 'Coronation Gold'. 'Moonshine' grows eighteen to twenty-four inches and is hardy from zone 3 to 7. 'Coronation Gold', at three feet, is one of the best achilleas for drying. These two are replacing the more massive 'Gold Plate'.

A new strain of achilleas, the Galaxy hybrids, come in a range of pastels — pink, salmon, cerise, and yellow — and a mixture of bright colors, including a rich dark red. As the flowers mature, they fade to paler tones, and they are particularly lovely in old-fashioned fresh and dried arrangements. The Galaxies are about two feet tall and spread from underground runners, as does one of their ancestor species, *A. millefolium,* or milfoil, a medicinal herb. Their dense, matlike foliage is finely cut and ferny, like that of milfoil.

The little woolly yarrow, *A. tomentosa,* makes an attractive groundcover for sunny places. Its dense silvery green foliage hugs the ground until midsummer, when the yellow, umbrella-form flowers shoot up on eight- to twelve-inch stems.

All the achilleas can be grown from seeds, cuttings, or vegetative divisions. They like sun or afternoon shade and will tolerate drought and dry soil (although they will grow better in good loam). They need good drainage. When you cut the flowers for drying, wait until they are fully open or the stems will go limp.

Agastache spp.
Giant hyssop, anise hyssop, Korean mint, mosquito plant

Except for one species, this genus is little known except to herb enthusiasts. But these are wonderful plants for garden color and for attracting hummingbirds, honeybees, and butterflies. Anise hyssop, *Agastache foeniculum,* the best-known species, has dark gray-green, licorice-scented foliage on erect, three- to four-foot-tall plants and numerous dense spikes of mauve flowers in late summer. It is native to the Great Plains of North America and became well known in Europe as a bee plant before it showed up in herb gardens here. It makes a handsome, long-blooming plant, perennial through zone 3 with mulching. It grows very well for me in zone 7 but is short-lived, probably because of the extreme heat. Volunteer plants spring up around the mother plant but are easy to hoe out.

A. rugosa, Korean mint, looks and smells somewhat like anise hyssop, but has more wrinkly leaves. It comes in white- and pink-flowered forms in addition to the wild purple form.

In warm climates, *A. mexicana,* Mexican giant hyssop, grows to five feet tall and has lemon-scented foliage. Its flowers are reddish purple and are borne in four-inch spikes. This herb has not been extensively tested for hardiness; I doubt if it can survive winters north of zone 8. Elsewhere, it can be grown as an annual if started early indoors from seeds and transplanted after frost danger.

One of the cold-hardiest of the agastaches is *A. cana,* or mosquito plant, a pink-flowered species native to high elevations of west Texas and southern New Mexico, where it survives low winter temperatures. Its two-foot plants are topped with loose spikes of pink flowers that are larger than those of the other species. This agastache looks best in drifts on hillsides. It needs very well-drained soil that remains fairly dry year-round.

All the agastaches are used for brewing teas and tisanes, for making piquant sauces for meats, and for drying to make potpourris.

Alchemilla spp.
Lady's mantle

The name *Alchemilla* should give you a clue that alchemy influenced the naming of this herb. The ancients knew of its styptic and astringent properties and used its leaves to stop bleeding. You will see lady's mantle planted in many herb gardens as an edging or ground-covering plant. It grows best in light shade in the North and moderate shade in the South and West. With snow cover, it will survive winters through zone 4.

Lady's mantle forms low, spreading plants that average six inches in height until they begin blooming, then push up to twelve inches in the sun, slightly higher in shade. The rounded, scalloped, hairy leaves seem to do magical things with moisture as they comb it from fog and capture condensation in crystal clear, reflective droplets.

Lady's mantle blooms in midsummer, when the plants glow with sprays of light greenish yellow blossoms, which last for six to eight weeks. These dry well for wreaths and potpourris.

You can buy plants of lady's mantle or grow them easily from seed in the spring. If you want to use the herb as a groundcover, you can get enough vegetative divisions from a few mother plants if you allow them a few months to grow.

One of the most beautiful herbs is 'Bergartten' sage, as shown by this single plant at the National Herb Garden, in Washington, D.C.

Allium spp.
Chives, silver chives, garlic, garlic chives, serpent garlic

Common chives, *Allium schoenoprasum,* are beautiful when they flower in April or May and attractive at other times. Use them for edgings or container plantings. Chives grow in closely packed clumps of hollow, tubular, onion-scented leaves from one-sixteenth to one-quarter inch in diameter. Established clumps send up leafless flowering stems to a height of sixteen inches. Colorful membranes cover the ball-like clusters of pink or lavender-pink blossoms, and split as they open. Chives are hardy through zone 4 in well-drained soil and tolerate summer heat fairly well. When we sold cut herbs, we sheared our chive plants flush with the ground after they flowered, and they grew back without yellow tips. Dig, divide, and reset clumps after three or four seasons. You can also direct-seed chives in nursery beds in early spring and transplant the seedlings to landscape sites in the fall.

Silver or corkscrew chives, *A. senescens* 'Glaucum', are grown for ornament rather than for the kitchen. This cultivar produces rather sparse twelve- to eighteen-inch plants with twisted silvery leaves. Despite its delicate appearance, it is hardy through zone 4.

Garlic chives, *A. tuberosum,* make plants twice as tall as common chives and bloom much later; their large, flattened clusters of clear white or lavender-pink flowers come in August, at a time when most perennial flowers have done their thing. In our herb fields, we noted that garlic chives were visited by more colorful harmless insects than any other plants except, perhaps, the mountain mints. Garlic chives are a valuable culinary plant; you can chop the flat dark green leaves to give a mild garlic flavor to salads and potatoes, and the flavorful flowers and seed nutlets make a decorative, edible garnish for salads. The dried skeletons of the flowers are valuable for arrangements. Garlic chives are very hardy, and spread rather rapidly by clump expansion and by dropped seeds. Police the plants to keep them from mugging neighboring herbs.

A variety of garlic, *A. sativum* var. *ophioscorodon,* rocambole or serpent garlic, makes a wonderful addition to herb gardens, prompting visitors to ask, "What is it?" Its bulbs are smaller and milder than those of common garlic, and its leaves are slenderer. What makes it such a curiosity is its coiled flower stems, which loosen into loops as the rather small flowers burst their scales. The plants display better if planted in groups where variations of the coiling and looping can heighten interest. Hardy through zone 5.

Aloysia triphylla
Lemon verbena

This shrubby, deciduous, half-hardy perennial is best known in the South and West, where it grows to a maximum height of eight feet. In zone 6 and north, where it must be grown as an annual, it may reach only two to three feet in height. Lemon verbena plants are open and billowy, and make good backgrounds for smaller herbs. The leaves are long, narrow, rough, and light green, keel-shaped in cross-section. Where summers are long and warm, frothy panicles on the tips of branches come in late summer.

Lemon verbena is such a valuable herb that gardeners in hardiness zone 7 cut the stems down to six-inch stubs and mulch the crowns with old boughs, pine straw, or leaves for winter protection. Don't remove the mulch until a week or two before the average spring frost-free date, and then gradually. Further north, take cuttings from the new summer growth that sprouts after stems have been pruned. The cuttings will strike roots in three to four weeks. Take them indoors (don't worry when they drop leaves, a natural occurrence) and keep them in a well-lighted area. They will sprout new leaves with the coming of late spring.

Use lemon verbena fresh in cookies, bread, teas, and stir-fries and dried in potpourris. The sweet, lemony flavor keeps reasonably well in the dried product.

Angelica spp.
Angelica

The angelicas are among the best tall biennial herbs for vertical accents. They are hardy and will survive zone 4 winters with mulch-

This five-foot-tall plant of 'Tuscan Blue' rosemary grows in the author's South Carolina garden.

141

ing. The green-stemmed *Angelica archangelica,* native to northern Europe, is the preferred culinary angelica; its stems can be stripped of strings and eaten raw or candied. The tall, ribbed stems support many flat clusters of greenish white flowers on five- to six-foot-tall plants.

If you want an even showier angelica, plant *A. gigas,* Korean angelica. It has glossy, reddish purple stems and rich purple flowers that contrast beautifully with its dark purple-green leaves. In rich soil it can grow to a height of eight feet.

The angelicas bloom in midsummer. They bear many large, spindle-shaped seeds, which, if planted right away, will germinate readily. Don't cover them; the seeds need light to germinate. For maximum production of flowers and tender stems, grow the plants in rich organic soil with afternoon shade. Angelica usually requires two years to bloom after seeds have germinated. You can prolong the life of the plants by clipping off the flower heads before they set seeds.

Artemisia spp.
Wormwood

Named for Artemis, the goddess of the chase, this enormous genus has contributed more gray-, silver-, and white-leaved herbs to gardens than any other. All have bitter-tasting, aromatic foliage and insignificant flowers, but dry easily and hold their foliage in wreaths.

My favorites among the artemisias are the landscaping selections that make mounded plants of finely cut silvery white foliage. They look fragile but can endure severe winters and hot summers if grown on well-drained soil. A hybrid of uncertain origin, 'Powys Castle', forms plants up to three feet high with ferny, twice-cut leaves of silvery green. Old plants look like wide-spreading shrubs. It will survive zone 4 winters with a deep mulch. The feathery-leaved *A. schmidtiana* 'Silver Mound' grows to one foot high and eighteen inches across. It also needs mulching in zone 4 and is more demanding of good soil conditions than larger, more robust artemisias.

Other good artemisias are the selections from beach wormwood,

A. stellerana, such as 'Silver Brocade'. The plants are low-growing and spreading, with whitish, felty, lobed leaves; sprays of yellow flowers come in late summer. Like 'Silver Mound', this little artemisia demands light soil to perform well all season.

If you want a large subshrub in the genus *Artemisia,* select one of the southernwoods, *A. abrotanum,* or old man. The unimproved species makes a dark silvery green plant with finely cut foliage and (to me) a rather rank camphorlike odor. Try the 'Tangerine' cultivar instead; it has a more pleasant scent. The southernwoods grow three feet tall and four feet across, and are hardy through zone 6.

A. ludoviciana 'Silver King', the compact 'Silver Queen', and the closely related 'Lambrook Silver' are among the most popular herbs for wreathmaking but are aggressive spreaders. Plant one of the well-mannered, mound-forming artemisias if you have a small garden.

Only one of the artemisias has important culinary uses, the anise-scented French tarragon, *A. dracunculus* var. *sativa.* Tarragon won't take any prizes for beauty; its plain green, narrow-leaved plants seldom flower, and when they do, they don't set seeds. It is a hardy perennial that survives zone 4 winters if grown in well-drained soil and mulched deeply. In the South and warm West, it doesn't live long and goes dormant for long periods under summer stress. If you have difficulty growing tarragon or persuading it to live through your winters, don't blame yourself; it is one of the most capricious herbs.

All the perennial artemisias can be multiplied easily by tip cuttings. Beware of recommendations for using the ornamental artemisias medicinally and as condiments; heavy or prolonged use can cause severe, irreversible poisoning. This is why absinthe is outlawed in most countries.

Ballota spp.
Ballota, false horehound, Greek horehound

Three species of the genus *Ballota* are gradually becoming available through herb nurseries. *Ballota pseudodictamnus* is a woolly, creamy gray plant with ascending branches. The flowers are small and white but are upstaged by the ornate greenish calyxes arranged in whorls around the flowering stems. Native to Mediterranean islands, *B. pseudodictamnus* is tender and except in very mild climates is grown as an annual. Its chief use is in hanging baskets, but I have seen it grown in the ground as a silver herb in warm western gardens.

B. acetabulosa is gray-green rather than cream-colored and turns silver at maturity. Its flowers are insignificant, but the persistent silvery calyxes are large and decorative. It too is tender and mostly used in hanging baskets. *B. acetabulosa* has limber stems that droop over the edges of baskets but don't trail. Both decorative species are propagated by softwood cuttings.

Ballota nigra, black horehound, should be avoided. Although it has some medicinal uses, it smells bad and spreads out of control if you turn your back on it.

Calamintha spp.
Calamint

Plant the *Calamintha* species here and there in your herb garden and you'll have visitors asking for starts of it. They are not spectacular plants; their flowers are small, but as numerous as those of summer savory. The dark green plants have small leaves and slender branches that move in the wind. Native to southern Europe, the calamints prefer well-limed soil. Surprisingly, they are hardy through zone 4. They flower in midsummer for me and come back every year.

C. nepeta grows to about eighteen inches on sandy soil in my sunny herb garden, but up to two feet in cooler areas. It has gray-green, pleasantly aromatic foliage reminiscent of mint, and whitish pink flowers that have a magnetic attraction for bees. The equally fragrant *C. grandiflora* has somewhat larger leaves and larger flowers, bright pink and showy. It likes moist sites and can tolerate light to moderate shade. Start from potted plants; a few herb specialists offer them.

Calocephalus brownii
Cushionbush

This is an eye-catching plant, so densely clothed with white wool that it looks ghostlike. It hasn't been grown much outside botanical gardens as yet, but it is so beautiful and unusual that it is bound to show up in the gardens of advanced herb enthusiasts before long. Cushionbush is native to Australia's warm, seasonally dry environment and will not overwinter in gardens north of zone 9. If you plant it in a container, grow it in a warm place outdoors during the summer, and take it indoors for the winter, however, it will grow into a small, handsome shrub. It can be kept in bounds by pruning. Look for it at plant sales sponsored by botanical gardens.

Capparis spinosa
Caper bush

In zones 9 and 10 you can grow this fascinatingly beautiful shrub as a landscape specimen. Elsewhere, grow it in containers in warm, protected corners and overwinter the plants indoors. Water the pots sparingly.

The familiar green capers harvested from the bushes are actually their flower buds, pickled and salted. Caper bushes grow to a maximum height of five feet, but except in virtually frost-free areas seldom exceed two feet. The large, long-stemmed pink or white flowers have long stamens that add to their beauty. The leaves are nearly round, and the canopy is rather open.

Plants are hard to find; grow caper bushes from seeds or tip cuttings. Seeds are very hard to germinate unless you nick the coat and sprout them at 75° to 80°F. You can grow caper bushes as a long-season annual if you start seeds very early indoors and grow the seedlings in pots under fluorescent lights. Shift the plants up to one-gallon, then three-gallon containers in midseason and place them against a sunny west- or south-facing wall, protected from the wind.

In zones 9 and 10, grow caper bushes on sandy soil and keep them on the dry side.

Ceanothus americanus
New Jersey tea

Erect, shrubby, flowering herbs of any species are useful in landscapes; New Jersey tea qualifies on all counts, and delivers bonuses. It has considerable value for medicines, teas, and dyes, and lovers of wildlife plant it for spring bloom — clouds of tiny insects are attracted to the oval clusters of creamy white blossoms on twig tips, and they provide food for the returning flights of insectivorous birds. New Jersey tea is hardy through the lower half of zone 4.

I have New Jersey tea in my wildflower garden, where it is shaded for half the day. My single plant is beginning to spread by shoots coming up from roots near the surface. It is rather plain and inconspicuous when not in bloom, but because of its late spring beauty and aromatic leaves, I would not be without it.

The plants seldom exceed three feet in height and two feet in spread. Propagate them by taking softwood cuttings from the new spring growth. Look around the plants and you may see seedlings coming up from dropped seeds, or suckers arising from roots. These can be potted up and transplanted after they have developed a strong root system.

Chamaemelum nobile
Roman chamomile

The soothing properties of chamomile tea were known long before it was prescribed for Peter Rabbit. The herb grew wild around the Mediterranean and was used in medicines and cosmetics by the ancients. Missionaries and traders took seeds of it all over Europe, where it naturalized readily.

Chamomile grows to about a foot tall and drops so many seeds that a springtime thinning of volunteers may be necessary. Technically, it is a perennial, but with so many volunteers, its longevity is a moot point. Chamomile foliage is apple-green and ferny; the yellow-

Three favorites — gold variegated sage, pineapple sage, and green santolina — display well against gray pea gravel.

centered, daisylike white flowers come in flushes as new plants mature. The plants are durable, and despite their apparent fragility can come back after being stepped on. The active ingredients in chamomile are concentrated in the flower heads, which are easy to harvest and dry.

A special nonflowering cultivar, 'Treneague', was developed for lawns in Great Britain; it is propagated vegetatively. While it makes a good groundcover for small areas, I wouldn't recommend attempting to plant a lawn with it in North America.

Chrysanthemum parthenium
Feverfew

Inexplicably, feverfew, one of the most efficacious of the medicinal herbs, carries no floral symbolism and little herbal lore from ancient days. No matter; its reputation as a garden flower is secure. The wild, three-foot-high, perennial European strain has small, single, daisylike flowers, but the improved, double-flowered cultivar is only one foot high and showier. To my eyes, it is one of the best white-flowered herbs available. It blooms in midsummer, when the white flowers nearly hide the foliage. They fade after two or three weeks, but if you shear them off and feed and water the plants, they will rebloom, providing the season is long enough. Shearing will prevent seeds from dropping and volunteering all over the place.

Start feverfew from seeds or cuttings. Cuttings root so readily, in only a week or two, that you can quickly create new plants. At the end of summer, set them out in the garden, and they will form a good root system before cold weather sets in. You can buy plants of golden feverfew, which has greenish yellow leaves, and of a curious yellow-flowered type that has no ray petals. Its flowers look like round yellow buttons. Feverfew is hardy through zone 4.

Echinacea spp.
Purple prairie coneflower

Several species of North American wildflowers are known as coneflowers. Of these, the echinaceas were an important part of the pharmacopia of native American tribes. Extracts have been used for many years in Europe for healing wounds and soothing insect stings, and health food stores now carry them in this country.

The purple prairie coneflower, *Echinacea purpurea,* grows wild in several states and is two to three feet tall, perhaps five feet on moist soil. It blooms in midsummer and grows more robust as the crown increases in size. Modern cultivars are hardy into zone 3 and have dark disks and purple, pink, or white ray petals. Flower diameters of four inches are not uncommon.

The most potent source of medicines, *E. angustifolia,* is a less showy species that has been subjected to heavy collection from the wild to meet European demand. The federally endangered pale coneflower, *E. pallida,* is also high in active compounds. It makes a most unusual garden flower, because its slender pinkish white petals hang down around the dark centers. The Tennessee coneflower, *E. tennesseensis,* which grows in only a small area in Tennessee, is also classified as federally endangered. Nurseries in states where endangered species are endemic are allowed to propagate and sell them within the state, but not elsewhere without special, hard-to-get permits.

The echinaceas grow rather easily from seeds but require two to three years to produce a significant show of color. You can buy plants of purple coneflower from most retail nurseries. Two-year-old container-grown plants will bloom soon after you plant them.

Foeniculum vulgare
Fennel

Two different-looking plants are known as fennel — the tall, yellow-flowered wild or sweet fennel herb and the shorter, "bulbing" Florence fennel or finocchio, which is considered a vegetable. Sweet fennel is one of the signature plants of herb gardens. You can recognize it from a distance; in fertile soil, it grows to six feet tall. It is native to Europe and has been one of the most popular culinary herbs throughout history. Charlemagne speeded its dispersal throughout Europe by ordering fennel planted in monastery gardens. Stalks and flower heads are eaten; seeds are chewed as a breath freshener.

This singularly lovely herb is silver-edged thyme. In cool weather, the twigs have a rose-pink blush.

To grow sweet fennel, sow seeds in the garden as soon as the soil can be worked in the spring. Sweet fennel is a biennial. Enjoy the first season's foliage in fish dishes; the plant will overwinter through zone 4 with snow cover, and will set lots of yellow, umbrella-like flowers the following summer. In all probability, seeds will drop and grow into replacement plants for the following year. At times sweet fennel does not die after flowering but regrows the following year. The plant looks a bit like dill, but has solid stems and a licorice aroma and taste.

Florence fennel, *F. vulgare* var. *azoricum,* also a biennial but grown as an annual, has broad, flat stalks. Where they emerge at the base, they swell to form what is commonly called a bulb, which is steamed and eaten as a vegetable, or served raw in salads as a crudité.

Galium odoratum
Sweet woodruff, waldemeister

You can use sweet woodruff to flavor May wine, to stuff mattresses, and to strew on floors. You can make it into a soothing tea or use it in potpourris or tussie-mussies, but what makes sweet woodruff valuable to gardeners is its potential as a sweetly scented groundcover in shady areas. It is one of the few herbs that not only tolerates light to moderate shade but actually performs better if given respite from the afternoon sun.

The green leaves of woodruff, tapered at both ends, are held in whorls like the spokes of a wheel. Borne on the tips of stems of even length, they form a dense mat about twelve inches high. Numerous clusters of clear white, fragrant flowers rise above the foliage in early summer.

The seeds of sweet woodruff apparently contain germination inhibitors, which retard germination and spread it over an extended period. For this reason, it is best to propagate the herb by taking sprouts that come up from the underground runners. Buy plants or check around established plants in late spring and you may find seedlings coming up from seeds dropped in previous years. Plants are hardy through zone 4.

Helichrysum spp.
Strawflower, curry plant, false licorice

Many helichrysums, including the everlasting strawflowers, are better known to gardeners, but curry plant, *Helichrysum angustifolium,* is an interesting novelty. It is a half-hardy perennial that can be grown as an annual in zone 6 and north. In my zone 7 garden, I have maintained a plant in a five-gallon container for three years, and it has suffered little or no winter damage. It is growing alongside a walk where I brush against it in passing. By no stretch of the imagination can curry plant replace the many exotic regional curries of India, but it does add a passable curry flavor to cooked dishes. Culinary properties aside, the plant itself is beautiful — two feet tall, silvery gray, with very fine needlelike leaves. In late summer you get a bonus from the loads of small yellow blossoms, which look like buttons. Grow curry plant from started plants or rooted tip cuttings.

Helichrysum petiolatum, false licorice, is an anise-scented gray herb with small, round, woolly leaves. It is not the source of licorice

for flavoring, but its handsome color, delicious aroma, and descending branches attract attention when the plants are used in hanging baskets and freestanding containers. It is a South African plant, tender and demanding of well-drained, well-limed soil. I've never seen it bloom; I understand that older plants set a heavy crop of creamy, showy bracts where summers are long. Many herb specialists offer plants of it.

Humulus spp.
Hop, hop vine

Dried hop flowers and bracts are used to add a slightly bitter taste to beer. Commercial production of hops from the European species, *H. lupulus,* is centered in the Willamette Valley of Oregon, which offers rather mild winters, cool nights, warm days, and abundant irrigation water. However, the plants will survive most winters in zone 4. Hops are one of the few vining herbs for training up posts and arbors; the vines have furry leaves that look a bit like maple or sweet gum foliage. They don't twine, and have to be trained up supports and tied in place.

You have your choice of vines with green foliage or those of a golden cultivar called 'Aureus'. Start hop vines from cuttings made from underground stems.

If European hops are too tender for your winters, try the Japanese species, *H. japonicus.* It is a half-hardy perennial but grows so rapidly from seeds that vines will grow eight to ten feet in one season. A variegated green and white variety is available; it is usually grown from tip cuttings. This species appeared in seed catalogs around the turn of the century, promoted as a fast-growing screen for porches.

Hyssopus officinalis
Hyssop

Hyssop is planted in many biblical herb gardens today, but scholars do not agree that the plant we call hyssop is the hyssop referred to in the Bible, which may have been a species of the genus *Origanum.*

Chives are among the most useful herbs and, when in bloom, among the most beautiful. The flowers are edible.

Nevertheless, *H. officinalis* was mentioned in ancient literature as a holy plant, and has long been used for medicines and as a bitter condiment.

Cultivars of hyssop with pink, rosy red, white, and violet-blue flower spikes are available, as is a dwarf form of the blue. The herb grows into a two-foot-high, aromatic subshrub in mild climates but freezes to the ground where winters are severe. It is hardy through zone 4.

Hyssop is one of the good old reliables in herb landscapes. It grows into dense, very dark green, rounded bushes. The ascending branches, clothed with narrow, willowlike leaves, are tipped in mid-summer with showy flower spikes that last for weeks. Buy plants or grow hyssop from seeds, cuttings, or vegetative divisions; it should bloom the second year from seeds. Grow it on well-limed, dry soil in full sun. Hyssop takes the heat of southern gardens very well, yet endures for years in northern plantings.

Laurus nobilis
Bay, bay laurel, bay tree

Several trees are known as bay, but *Laurus nobilis* is the commercial source of bay leaves, well known for seasoning. It isn't hardy north of zone 8, and even there freezes to near the ground during occasional severe cold snaps. In most gardens, bay grows no larger than the herbaceous plants around it, and it has long been valued as a container plant.

The multiple-trunk bay beside my back steps is now four years old and about seven feet tall. Cold weather froze the branches back about two feet a year ago, but I pruned them in the spring and they regrew vigorously. Following cold weather, some of the green bleaches out of the leaves and the stems turn reddish brown, but with the return of warm weather and a good feeding, the tree resumes its normal deep green color.

In more severe climates, grow bay in large containers. Move them outdoors during warm weather and take them indoors before the first frost. Bay laurel makes a beautiful plant that responds to pruning by becoming denser. With yearly shifting up to successively larger containers, your bay tree will before long grow too large for one person to move. That's the time to offer it to a botanical garden or to a church or office building with a sunny indoor site for plants.

Lavandula spp.
Lavender and lavandin

Lavender may well be the single most popular fragrant herb for landscaping and craft use. It has everything one could wish for in an herb: delightful fragrance, fresh or dried; silvery gray foliage; long spikes of blue, pink, or white flowers; and drought-resistance. Lavender has been honored through the ages as exemplifying virtue, and in more recent generations it has been prized as an ingredient in soaps, lotions, and cosmetics — nostalgia, distilled and captured.

Early Greeks and Romans took plants of various lavender species across Europe, where a process of natural selection set in so that varieties of one species, *Lavandula angustifolia,* developed a moderate degree of winter-hardiness. Much later, when the perfume industry developed, growers began a continuing process of hybridizing for lavender oil content and quality rather than for hardiness. Gradually, the half-hardy hybrids came to be commonly known as lavandins, or technically as *Lavandula* × *intermedia.* Breeders created them by crossing *L. angustifolia* with *L. latifolia.* Spanish, Dutch, and English lavender came to represent the particular blends of lavandin oils coming from those geographical areas.

L. angustifolia, commonly but erroneously called English lavender, contains the hardiest of the well-known cultivars, including 'Munstead', 'Hidcote', 'Twickel Purple', and the recently introduced 'Montana Blizzard'. With snow cover, these vegetatively propagated cultivars are hardy through zone 5. 'Hidcote' has been known to survive zone 4 winters if heavily mulched. Plants labeled *L. spica* or *L. vera* have been grown from seeds of *L. angustifolia* and may not be reliably hardy.

Hardy plants grown from cuttings taken from accurately named cultivars of *L. angustifolia* can be obtained from better nurserymen and herb specialists. The cultivars differ mostly in plant height, foliage color, flower color, and, to a limited extent, fragrance. The height of established plants under good culture depends on the length and average temperature of the growing season and the severity of winters. 'Munstead', for example, might grow three feet high in northern California but only half that high in Pennsylvania. Dwarf cultivars, which have shorter internodes between leaves, grow only about half as high as their parent stock.

Gardeners along the West Coast and in low elevations of the Southwest often grow the half-hardy species lavenders and lavandin hybrids to get a wider range of foliage types, blossom forms, colors, and aromas. In more trying climates you can grow these plants as annuals, either buying new plants each year or taking cuttings and overwintering them as houseplants. If you wish to grow lavender from seed, expect poor or fair but uneven germination, extending over a month or two. All the lavenders do reasonably well as houseplants if grown by a west- or south-facing window or beneath a fluorescent light, and not overwatered.

Harvest lavender spikes as soon as they have bloomed, bundle the stems, and hang them in the dark to dry—and be sure to provide good ventilation to keep the interior stems from molding. After the plants have bloomed, prune off leggy branches to dry for sachets and potpourris. Pruning will encourage more branching and denser plants. In heavy soil, lavender grows better if planted on low mounds and mulched with one inch of white sand. It's not a good idea to mulch lavender crowns with leaves, wood chips, or pine straw for winter protection, since these can cause the crowns to rot during rainy winters.

Lobelia siphilitica
Great blue lobelia

At one time, great blue lobelia was used to treat syphilis. Although it was not up to that awesome challenge, the plant does qualify as an herb, and you will often see its beautiful blue spikes in herb gardens, where light to medium shades of blue are rare.

I have several plants of great blue lobelia in my wildflower meadow, where they bloom in late summer. In my dry soil, the plants grow to a height of two feet, but they will reach three feet in moist locations that are shaded in the afternoon. The rather large, open-faced flowers are tightly packed on racemes, and they must set lots of seeds, because I find volunteers in sandy spots around the mother plants.

Great blue lobelia is a hardy perennial and will survive winters in zone 4. It grows well in full sun in the North but prefers afternoon shade in the South. White-flowered plants occasionally show up in populations grown from seeds, and a dwarf cultivar is available — though I have no idea why anyone would want a shorter version of such a stately flower.

Lobelia seeds are unbelievably tiny, as fine as dust. One way to germinate them is to scatter them over a pot of seed-starting mix that has been topped with one-eighth inch of milled sphagnum moss.

Two very popular cultivars of sage, gold variegated and tricolor, are often used in containers and knot gardens.

'Moonshine' is the most popular yellow yarrow. See how its flowers, just opening, agree with the bronze-purple of *Salvia superba* 'East Friesland'.

Herb gardeners love old-fashioned wild or pot marjoram, which is actually an oregano, for its easy-to-dry, long-stemmed flowers. It has little or no fragrance or flavor.

Water the pot from the bottom to avoid washing the seeds around. They will gravitate down in the sterile moss and do not need to be covered. They usually come up in clumps and are transplanted as such. Separate the seedlings during the second transplanting, three or four weeks later, when they have formed strong root systems and can be pulled apart.

Marrubium spp.
Horehound

Common white horehound, *Marrubium vulgare,* is perennial through zone 4. It has a camphorlike odor and is grown mostly to flavor medicine and candy. Common horehound isn't as showy as silver horehound, *M. incanum,* which has woolly white leaves and interesting, chaffy flower heads threaded on the stems; it forms spreading plants fifteen inches high. Silver horehound is marginally hardy and is best carried over winter indoors in zone 6 and north; take cuttings from branch tips in late summer. It grows well in containers but is a bit rough-looking compared with false horehound, *Ballota acetabulosa,* a different species (see page 144).

Melissa officinalis
Lemon balm, sweet balm, cure-all

We use lemon balm primarily as a culinary herb and secondarily as a landscape plant. It is a particularly athletic member of the mint family, given to jumping edgings and burrowing under obstacles. For that reason, grow it in bottomless five-gallon buckets or lengths of chimney flue tile. Despite these precautions, it may still spread; it also volunteers enthusiastically from dropped seeds.

Lemon balm grows eighteen to thirty inches high and is reliably hardy through zone 5. Juvenile plants have a nice upstanding form, but they soon flop and begin spreading. The flowers are white and nondescript. I much prefer one of the colorful selections of lemon balm to the plain green variety, either the green and white 'Variegata' or the greenish gold 'Aurea'. Buy plants of these; they must be grown from vegetative divisions or they will revert to green. Grow the green variety from seeds or cuttings.

Lemon balm is good in teas and in mint sauces for meats. Tender young leaves can be chopped and sprinkled on salads or rubbed on the bowl to impart a lemony aroma and tangy taste. Lemon balm loses some of its flavor in drying but can be frozen successfully.

Mentha spp.
Mint, spearmint, peppermint, et al.

Whenever I encounter an herb that is new to me, the first thing I do is check the stem near the base. If the stem is square in cross section, it is a member of the mint family, which includes genera as diverse as the culinary mints, the salvias, and the basils.

The culinary mints, genus *Mentha,* are such aggressive spreaders and require so much water that it is best to grow them in the vegetable garden, where you can keep them under control. If they escape, you can dig them out without disturbing a carefully planned herb garden. If you want to use them in landscapes, grow them in bottomless five-gallon buckets sunk in the ground to leave a two-inch rim protruding, or in eighteen-inch lengths of chimney flue liner. Set a necklace of walnut-size stones two deep around the rim of the container, to discourage the cross-country runners from hurdling the top and taking root.

A good strain of spearmint, *Mentha spicata,* has so many culinary uses that you should have at least one plant of it in your herb garden, but black peppermint, *M. × piperata,* has darker green foliage and makes a stronger statement in landscapes. Pineapple mint, *M. suaveolens* var. *variegata,* is a robust cream and white variegated plant that looks good in landscapes. A variegated peppermint, *M. × piperata* 'Variegata', has a more distinct contrast between its clear white and deep green colors, but it is particular about soil conditions. It often mysteriously reverts to solid green, and when a solid white branch appears, it usually turns brown and dies because it lacks chlorophyll.

You can find dozens of mint cultivars listed in herb specialty catalogs, all with different aromas. They look a lot alike, except the ones with curly or variegated leaves. If part of your herb garden is in light to moderate shade, try orange bergamot mint; it has large purple- or bronzy green leaves and a pleasant but indescribable aroma somewhat like that of *Monarda didyma.*

English pennyroyal, *M. pulegium,* is a handsome, low-growing, strongly scented, insect-repellent plant that with sufficient moisture can tolerate light to medium shade. It resembles peppermint but has much smaller leaves, stays lower, and is hardy through zone 5. I'm not bothered by contact with it, but one of the workers on our herb farm broke out in blisters when she rubbed the juice of fresh pennyroyal on her skin to repel insects.

All of the mints should be propagated by tip cuttings or by lengths of their fleshy roots. They will grow from seeds, but their offspring will be highly variable.

Monarda spp.
Bergamot, bee balm, Oswego tea, lemon mint

No other herb can draw as many hummingbirds to gardens as the red-flowered bergamot, *Monarda didyma.* For a solid month in midsummer, bergamot attracts hummingbirds from afar with its whorls of dark red, tubular flowers atop four-foot-high stems. At other seasons the reddish bronze foliage makes an attractive tall background in herb gardens and perennial borders.

Bergamot comes in several colors: red, purple, pink, white, and intermediate shades. It is native to moist, sunny swales in the eastern United States; I have seen it blooming amid underbrush along roadsides in the Blue Ridge Mountains.

Somewhere in the process of plant selection, breeders diminished the natural resistance of bergamot to mildew disease, but they now are introducing new selections with strong resistance. If your plants suffer from this disfiguring condition, you can minimize it by removing two of every three stems in a clump, which will allow better air circulation.

Monarda didyma is hardy through zone 4; it dies down at the end of the season and sends up new stems from underground runners. Small potted plants purchased and planted in the spring sometimes don't blossom until the following season.

A similarly hardy native North American bee balm, *Monarda fistulosa,* comes in lavender pink and occasionally white blossom forms. Its plants are a bit slenderer and the whorls of flowers are smaller than those of *M. didyma.* It rarely contracts mildew.

A third monarda, *M. citriodora,* confusingly called lemon mint, is an annual or biennial native to the South, but it is rapidly appearing in herb gardens all over the country. It has camphor-scented, not lemony, foliage. Its season of bloom depends on the latitude of the garden; in zones 8 and 9 it germinates in the fall, makes good-size vegetative rosettes during the winter, and blooms in early summer. Further north, seeds germinate in the spring and blooms come in late summer. In my wildflower meadow, lemon mint grows about two feet high and blooms on several whorls threaded on the top third of the erect stem. The flowers are dark pink with purple spots. The plants are rather sparse and look best if planted close together in drifts. I get the most volunteer plants on patches of sandy soil where I have limed to a pH of 6.0.

Myrrhis odorata
Sweet cicely, sweet chervil

Anise-scented sweet cicely is perennial through zone 5; further north, grow it as an annual or biennial. The plants are pretty and feathery, with thin, ferny leaves and branching umbels of white flowers in early summer. The leaves look a bit like those of chervil. A native of Europe, it has escaped to the wild in the eastern part of the country but has not become a nuisance. Sweet cicely forms heavy black roots in moist, fertile soil and grows to a height of two to three feet. Add the stems to cooked fruit or chop the leaves as a topping for salads, or add the leaves to bouquets garnis for seasoning meats. Sweet cicely grows easily from its large, ribbed seeds, which should be sown soon after harvest to insure good germination. Grow it in full sun or along woodland edges in the North, and in afternoon shade in the South and West.

Nepeta spp.
Catmint, catnip

The name *catmint* is often confused with *catnip*. Even though the plants belong to the same genus, they don't look much alike. Of the two, the refined catmints are much more popular for landscaping; the tall, coarse catnip is best for teas and for getting cats high. The hardy perennial catmints have spreading plants with many ascending branches tipped with spikes of paired pink, white, or lavender-blue flowers. The leaves are rough-textured, gray-green, and toothed, and may be shaped either like hearts or like teardrops, depending on the species. The lavender-flowered dwarf catmint, *Nepeta mussinii,* is the most popular species, because it seldom exceeds one foot in height and can tolerate neglect and dry soil. The hybrid *Nepeta* × *faassenii* can reach two feet in height; it also tolerates dry soil. *Nepeta grandiflora* has dark purple flowers, dark bracts, and larger leaves than other species. All the catmints can take light shade and can be grown from cuttings or divisions. They reproduce fairly true to type when grown from seeds. *N. mussinii* is the hardiest of the three; it will survive most winters in zone 4.

Ocimum basilicum
Sweet basil; common, cinnamon, lemon, and anise-scented basil

The basils make up one of the largest genera and are by far the most popular genus of kitchen herbs. They have been cultivated for so long that they have become part of the cuisine of many countries, and also the stuff of legends. Could it be because of the saying that the way to a man's heart is through his stomach that basil's significance in folklore often has a lot to do with love?

While some varieties grow into coarse, ungainly plants better suited for the food garden, other basils make excellent landscape

plants. The basils are native to the dry tropics of the Old World and must be grown as warm-weather annuals in North America, except in zones 9 and 10. They will continue to grow throughout the summer if the blossoms are trimmed off before they set seeds.

'Spicy Globe' is the best known of the ornamental basils. It forms wide-spreading, foot-high mounds of densely branched light green foliage with the typical peppery-clove basil scent, and is much used for edging herb or flower beds. Another variety of similar foliage and form but tinged purple is sold under a number of cumbersome names, such as *Ocimum basilicum minimum purpurascens* (its name in the Well-Sweep catalog), but you can recognize it by its tiny leaves and purple foliage.

Two large-leaved purple basils, 'Dark Opal' and 'Purple Ruffles', are often used for color accents in herb gardens. Maintain a good

Easily the most popular aromatic herb and a landscaping essential, lavender comes in species and hybrids that have blue, purple, pink, or white flowers and several different fragrances.

level of nitrogen in the soil when growing these two, as they turn bronze when nitrogen is deficient.

Rather recent introductions to the basil line, 'Cinnamon' and 'African Blue', grow into large, dark, attractive plants suitable for landscape accents or for seven-gallon or larger containers. 'Cinnamon' is notable for its purple bracts, lavender flowers, and dark stems; 'African Blue', for its rounded leaves streaked with darker veins and for its slowness to flower. Both grow to considerable size in warm climates — up to four feet tall in my garden. Anise-scented basil looks a bit like cinnamon basil but has taller, more open plants and thinner, toothed leaves. If you need a tall dark green herb that is rather cylindrical in form, consider 'Greek Column' basil. Its branches turn up sharply to make a slim, columnar plant.

All these basils can be used in place of common sweet basil in cooking, except 'Cinnamon,' which has such a pronounced cinnamon aroma that it is better used freshly chopped as a topping for baked squash, pumpkin, or sweet potato pie, and anise-scented basil. To harvest basil at peak flavor, select the tip ends of branches that have just begun to form flower bracts, before the first flowers begin to open. If you wish to dry them, place the tips in the refrigerator. When they have wilted, hang them in a dark, dry, well-ventilated place. The wilting removes moisture quickly and prevents the blackening that can occur in drying. (See pp. 123–26 for more on preserving basil.)

If you want just a bit of basil for fresh use, buy plants, but if you want to use the herb for ornamental plantings or for freezing, drying, and making pesto, you can grow it easily from direct-seeding. Delay planting until the soil is warm to your touch. Firm the seeds thoroughly into the soil so that they don't squirt out and try to germinate on top.

Origanum spp.
Oregano, sweet marjoram, dittany of Crete

A multitude of edible and ornamental herbs belong to the genus *Origanum,* including the many oreganos, sweet marjoram, and dit-

Wonderful new colors are available in the hybrid milfoil yarrows: crimson, pink, near-scarlet, yellow, cream, and bicolors, all on long stems. *Salvia* 'East Friesland' looks good with them, too.

tany of Crete. The oreganos grow wild in several countries around the Mediterranean and are among the most ancient of culinary herbs. They are very easy to dry and store and are simple to grow from seeds.

When we were supplying restaurants with fresh herbs, Italian oregano, *O. × majoricum,* a half-hardy hybrid, was our most popular cultivar. It is a clump-forming, white-flowered, sterile oregano with a warm, mild flavor. Greek oregano, *O. vulgare* subsp. *hirtum,* a much stronger-flavored and hardier oregano, came in a distant second in popularity. Neither of these is any great shakes for landscaping.

The rugged, hardy old *Origanum vulgare* is perennial through zone 5. It has long-stemmed dark purple flowers that are excellent for drying but doesn't offer much in the way of flavor. Four years after we closed our herb farm, it continues to survive and spread in the abandoned fields. The dwarf *O. vulgare* var. *humile* makes good flowering edgings. It isn't a rampant spreader and is hardy through zone 4.

A group of hybrid oreganos with the species *O. rotundifolium* as a parent, known mostly in Europe, make lovely landscape plants. They grow into slender, open plants with arching flower stems about a foot high. These support pinkish green, overlapping bracts that look something like rattlesnake buttons. The flowers themselves are inconspicuous, but the bracts are highly ornamental. The most notable of this group is the hybrid 'Kent Beauty', which requires a good level of lime in the soil and perfect drainage for optimum performance. Buy started plants of it. Its hardiness is still being evaluated; it would probably survive winters in zone 6.

Golden oregano, *O. vulgare* subsp. *vulgare* 'Aureum', is a pretty thing. It is not reliably hardy north of zone 7. In the South and West it tends to become sunburned if not given afternoon shade.

Sweet marjoram, *Origanum majorana,* a dainty, slow-growing little plant, is of minor landscape value but should be grown for its many uses in cooking. You can distinguish it from the plants known as oregano by its beaded flower buds and seed heads, its characteristic leaf shape and blue-green color, and the distinctive sweetness of its aroma. Except in California and the Deep South, sweet marjoram has to be grown as an annual.

Dittany of Crete, *O. dictamnus,* is beloved by herb enthusiasts. It is a creeping gray plant with fuzzy foliage that tops out at six to eight inches. It needs perfect drainage; plant it in hanging baskets or chink it into east- or north-facing walls, where it is protected from the afternoon sun. It is hardy through zone 6 with snow cover.

Harvest the edible oreganos and sweet marjoram by taking tender tips soon after the morning sun has dried the dew on leaves. Both dry quickly, but the flavor of the dried product lacks the subtlety of fresh leaves.

Pelargonium spp.
Scented geraniums

Whoever started calling these pelargoniums "geraniums" forever confused the issue, because they look and act nothing like the genus *Geranium.* However, those people really started something big; just by ordering two or three catalogs, you can take your pick from hundreds of cultivars of scented geraniums. Herb gardens with scented geraniums are beloved by visitors, who love to pinch and snip and perhaps beg a cutting or two. I like the way that Sandy Mush Herb Farm categorizes scented geraniums in six groups in order to simplify selection: rose-scented, lemon-scented, fruit- and spice-scented, mint-scented, pungent, and oak-leaved. Most of the cultivars are selections from about a dozen pelargonium species or hybrids between them. Some of the fragrances are blends of two or more essences — rose and cinnamon, for example.

Scented geraniums can be grown from seeds but usually don't come true to type. Customarily, they are grown from plants that are produced from cuttings or by micropropagation (meristem or tissue culture). They grow best in full sun on raised beds of sandy or sandy loam soil, with soil fertility kept on the slightly lean side to intensify fragrances. The citrus-scented cultivars from *P. crispum* have small, crinkled leaves and adapt particularly well to being trained into tree forms and grown in containers.

I have had robust scented geraniums such as rose-cinnamon live through mild winters here in zone 7, but I prefer to take no chances, and I propagate a few replacements by rooting tip cuttings in late summer. Many gardeners grow scented pelargoniums in pots as houseplants and move them outside after frost danger is past.

Perovskia atriplicifolia
Russian sage

Until about a decade ago, this plant was seldom seen except in the gardens of collectors of perennials. Then herb enthusiasts discovered its sagelike odor and began planting it for tall accents in herb gardens. Now it is extremely popular. Russian sage is one adaptable plant, able to survive winters in zone 4 and summers in zone 8! The gray plants grow to a height of three to four feet, are open and airy, and break into a great show of sprays of small lavender-blue blossoms in midsummer. They stay in color for several weeks. Grow from seeds or tip cuttings, or buy plants.

Petroselinum crispum
Parsley

Long before anyone knew about vitamins and their value in nutrition, people were planting parsley for its taste. Theophrastus described two types in 322 B.C., leaf and turnip-rooted. In all probability, both the tops and the roots of turnip-rooted parsley were first harvested from the wild and used in cooking. Later, to overcome the sparse production of leaves, growers developed plain-leaved selections of leaf parsley, and finally curly-leaved selections for salads and for decorating plates. Soil and sand are easy to wash off plain-leaved parsley, and its taste reputedly holds better in cooking than that of the curly-leaved varieties.

Parsley is one of the most companionable of plants, useful with annual and perennial flowers, as an edging for beds of ornamentals,

Two popular artemisias are used in this edging: Roman wormwood (left) and 'Silver Mound' (right). Behind them are the purple blossoms of Allium senescens and the yellow flowers of sweet fennel.

and in containers. It is a true biennial, and when flower stems shoot up on overwintered plants, you know it's the beginning of their end, as they will soon flower, set seeds, and die. In zone 7b and south, parsley remains green during the winter and can be harvested sparingly for garnishing and flavoring.

You can grow parsley from seeds, but because the seeds require three weeks to germinate and grow slowly for several more weeks, most gardeners buy plants. The herb will tolerate light shade in the North, and grows much better with afternoon shade in the South and warm West. Harvest parsley by snapping off the outer stems with a twisting motion. If you need large amounts for drying, shear off the entire plant two inches above the ground. New leaves will come from buds near the center of the crown.

'Silver Mound' requires a bit more care and better soil, and grows more slowly, than other artemisias, but it is so beautiful and silvery soft that hardly an herb garden is without it.

Phlomis fruticosa
Jerusalem sage

Jerusalem sage has erect plants up to four feet in height, with coarse, woolly, gray-white leaves. In early summer, later in the North, whorls of yellow flowers shaped like dog claws adorn the upper stems. It is an altogether pretty plant, and will bring praise from visitors to your garden. Grow it in full sun on rather dry soil. In coastal California, this tender perennial will come back from the roots in the spring. It will survive zone 8 winters if mulched lightly with pine straw. Elsewhere, you must grow it as an annual; north of zone 6, set out rather large plants in order to have them flower before frost.

Plectranthus spp.
Cuban oregano, Puerto Rican oregano, Vicks plant

Listed in many catalogs as *Coleus amboinicus,* Cuban or Puerto Rican oregano doesn't remotely resemble the oreganos in the genus *Origanum.* The sprawling plants have aromatic, medium-size, heavily felted, fleshy leaves and look good in containers or hanging baskets. The unimproved species has gray-green leaves, but the most popular cultivar is variegated cream and gray-green. The branch tips have long been used in Southeast Asia for flavoring foods, and more recently have been adopted in the Caribbean tropics, where the Mediterranean oreganos don't grow well. Grow Cuban oregano as an annual, as it is quite tender to frost. Tip cuttings root easily and can be carried over winter as houseplants.

Another plectranthus is grown as an herb: the so-called menthol plant or Vicks plant, which some growers sell as *Plectranthus marrubioides,* others as *P. purpuratus,* and still others as *P. caeruliae.* More confusion in names, but there is no mistaking the strong medicinal smell of the plant. It is sold as a houseplant but will grow well outdoors in hanging baskets, where its furry, fleshy leaves help it to shrug off stress from dryness. The plant is tender; dig it and pot it up for overwintering.

Poterium sanguisorba
Burnet, salad burnet

I have a soft spot in my heart for this decorative little culinary herb, because I've seen it used in so many landscaping situations and kitchen gardens. It isn't all that useful in the kitchen, but before your garden cucumbers are ready and after they have gone out of production, you can chop burnet to add a cucumber flavor to salads and drinks. Where burnet excels is in edgings; spaced eighteen inches apart, the plants form uncrowded lines of low green mounds. Individual plants look good too, particularly against rock or tufa mulches. The flowers on long, nearly leafless stems are not conspicuous, but the chaffy-looking green seed heads are attractive. Burnet is hardy through zone 5, but unless you divide it, it doesn't live long. Grow it from seeds or plants in full sun, and with moderate amounts of water and plant nutrients to maintain good foliage color.

Pycnanthemum spp.
Mountain mint

The mountain mints, handsome plants now grown mostly in wildflower meadows, are strongly scented members of the mint family native to various regions of North America. Herb gardeners are just learning how to use them for teas and potpourris, but the mountain mints can perform another important function in your garden with no help from you. In my wildflower meadow, I have noted that all four species of *Pycnanthemum* I grow attract not only bees and butterflies but an incredible variety of colorful and nonaggressive wasps. All season long I have worked around the plants and I have never been stung, even when harvesting branches for flower arrangements. Wasps are important factors in the pollination of native wildflowers, trees, and shrubs, and it behooves all of us to help them survive by providing food sources.

I grow *P. muticum, P. incanum, P. virginianum,* and *P. flexuosum.* Of these, I prefer *P. muticum* for landscaping. It grows into large clumps of robust stems three feet tall. Its sizable oval leaves are rather glossy, and turn from green to silvery gray in midsummer, with the silver especially intense at the branch tips. The pale pink to white flowers are not conspicuous and are clustered at the branch tips, where wasps, bees, and butterflies can get at them easily. *P. flexuosum* makes much smaller plants with slender leaves. You can tuck them here and there in herb gardens, unlike *P. muticum,* which should be used as a tall specimen plant.

Start the mountain mints from potted plants, or get starts from fellow herb enthusiasts. They grow easily from divisions sliced off the strong, thickety clumps. In good soil, these herbs are aggressive spreaders. *P. muticum* and *P. flexuosum* survive winters through zone 4. *P. pilosum* might survive through zone 5; Richters, an Ontario herb grower, offers it, and Richters leans toward the hardier species.

Rosmarinus officinalis
Rosemary

If rosemary were a ship, it long ago would have sunk under the load of baggage it has carried through the ages. The earliest philosophers and plantsmen mentioned it; biblical stories of Mother Mary's debt to rosemary abound; medieval gardeners depended on it to keep away evil spirits. Even today, a sprig of rosemary in a letter or a gift says more clearly than words that you remember that person with affection.

Early on, rosemary spread all over the Mediterranean basin, gradually moving north with evangelizing monks until it could no longer survive the winters. Then, so strong was its mystical appeal and so manifold its uses that gardeners built limestone walls to shelter it and give it the excellent drainage and sweet soil it prefers. We know rosemary as a strong, resinous flavoring for beef, chicken, and savory dishes. Back then, it was also strewn to mask odors, dried for scenting, used to season sausage, and cooked with gamy meats to disguise their heavy taste and smell.

Beyond its many culinary uses, rosemary offers all-season beauty, especially during early winter in the South and West, when it flowers heavily. In cooler climates it flowers in mid- to late summer. Its

Common chives and woolly yarrow in bloom provide a late spring burst of color. Blue catmint pushes up among fallen rose petals in the background.

blossoms are important to bees when other plants are dormant or out of flower.

Rosemary grows best in low-elevation gardens in California and the Southwest, and second best in hardiness zones 7 and 8 in the South. Along the Gulf Coast it suffers from high humidity and foliage diseases. There, all of the rosemaries are short-lived. North of hardiness zone 7a, only the hardiest cultivars, such as 'Arp' and 'Salem', will survive most winters; the creeping varieties are especially tender. If rosemary freezes in your garden, take the hint and move your plants indoors during the winter.

I have several large, erect plants of 'Arp', 'Tuscan Blue', and a nameless creeping rosemary that have lived through three mild winters in my garden. They grow against a south-facing wall and are mulched with large stones, which I hope will act as solar heat banks and protect them from perishing during an extremely cold winter. Across the South, damage from foliage diseases and root rots that start during humid summer weather kills almost as many rosemary plants as extreme winter cold.

Despite its marginal winter hardiness, rosemary is basic to herb landscapes. It can grow from a small plant in a four-inch pot to a significant dark gray-green plant eighteen inches tall and equally broad, in a rather short growing season. In zones 4, 5, and 6, most gardeners grow it as a container plant and overwinter it in the sunlight streaming through a sunny south- or west-facing window. Residents of dark homes or apartments grow it under fluorescent lights. More than any other herb, rosemary increases in real and sentimental value with age and is worth the trouble of winter protection indoors.

Rosemary adapts well to shaping into small pot-grown topiaries. Tom DeBaggio of Arlington, Virginia, is among the many commercial herb growers who train rosemary into "Christmas trees," baskets with handles, topiary trees, and other fanciful shapes for sale during the holiday season. Large creations require more than one season of growth in short-summer areas.

Buy plants or grow rosemary from cuttings. Seeds start slowly and germinate erratically. The soil should be well drained and of pH

6.0 to 7.5. When we operated Wilson's Savory Farm, we limed our acid soil according to soil test recommendations but did not remember that agricultural ground limestone reacts slowly. Consequently, our rosemary plants sulked until we mixed fast-acting pelleted limestone into the surface two inches of soil around the plants. (Note: liming is not required in the western states, except in coastal plateau areas where high rainfall creates acid soil.)

Rosemary comes with white, pink, and deep blue blossoms as well as the conventional light blue. You can buy cultivars with golden leaves, twisted branches, and needlelike pine-scented leaves. The erect rosemaries, such as 'Tuscan Blue', have considerably larger, broader leaves than the bushy types. Mass marketers who sell rosemary plants seldom market them by cultivar name but sell cutting-grown plants of ordinary bushy types that have not been selected for hardiness. You are better off dealing with a nursery or herb specialist who labels by cultivar name.

Ruta graveolens
Rue, herb of grace

Knowing what we do now about the ability of rue to cause severe contact dermatitis in some people, it is hard to imagine that its branches were once used to sprinkle holy water over the heads of sinners. Rue is one of many herbs supposed by the ancients to have magical powers.

Contemporary gardeners plant rue for its unique blue-green color and curiously lobed leaves, but in a few Baltic countries, the leaves are chopped and used sparingly on salads and sandwiches to give them a bitter tang. (Remind me to steer clear of those countries; just standing next to rue when it is in early bloom will make me break out in a rash, and I'm not bothered by poison ivy or poison oak.)

Rue is a pretty plant all season long. It is a long-lived, erect perennial that sets large numbers of yellow blossom clusters atop the plants in early summer. It is hardy through zone 4 but can die out if the soil is saturated for long periods during the winter. Old plants grow to about thirty inches high in my garden, and the stiff, deep-rooted plants stand up well through summer thunderstorms. You can buy a low-growing, spreading form for containers, but the dwarf 'Blue Mound' makes a better edging plant. There is also a variegated cultivar. Rue grows easily from seeds, but the plants will vary a bit in size and form. Most gardeners buy plants.

Salvia spp.
Sage

The genus *Salvia* is enormous, diverse, and dispersed over much of the world. The flowers of garden sage, *Salvia officinalis,* have long symbolized domestic virtue, an understandable connection, considering the versatility of the herb as a seasoning. Few of the other salvias, however, have been offered long enough to become saturated with symbolism.

Garden sage makes a beautiful gray-green, spreading plant one to two feet in height, with somewhat taller spikes of purple flowers. A dwarf version has compact plants with small leaves; plant them close together for edgings. Garden sage is a short-lived perennial, hardy through zone 4. In zone 7 and south it is prone to nematode damage and many root and foliage diseases, and is usually grown as an annual. Of the many varieties, my choice for landscaping is 'Bergartten', which has nearly round, thick leaves with contrasting veins. It makes a mounded plant like an overturned kettle; the leaves overlap, which creates a look of solidity. *S. officinalis* also includes the bicolored golden sage, purple sage, and tricolor sage. These three beauties are edible, but not quite as good nor as hardy as the gray-leaved garden sages. They are often used in knot gardens.

Other than *S. officinalis,* the herb salvias include the several species with fruit-scented foliage: grape-scented, *S. tarahumara;* apple, *S. pomifera;* dwarf pineapple-scented, *S. elegans* 'Frieda Dixon'; peach-scented, *S. dorisiana;* grapefruit-scented, *S. gesneriflora;* and 'Honeydew Melon', a *Salvia elegans* cultivar. All of these are treated as annuals north of zone 8. All grow into large plants that need occasional pruning to keep them neat. You might wish to try them

Winter tarragon, or anise-scented marigold, smells strongly and pleasantly of licorice. The tiny edible flowers come late in the season and are borne in great profusion.

'Blue Wonder' is an early-blooming, powerfully fragrant heliotrope.

in your food garden before moving them into landscape situations. Their fragrance is most intense on warm, humid, windless days.

Some of the fragrant herb species native to the Southwest have been used for flavoring — autumn sage, *S. greggii,* for one. Plant breeders have selected several colors from *S. greggii* which are proving to be neat, heat-resistant, showy flowers for late summer. They are perennial in my garden but not much further north, I suspect.

Another class of salvias that are irreplaceable in landscapes is those grown principally for massive silvery gray foliage. Clary sage, *S. sclarea;* silver sage, *S. argentea;* and Ethiopian sage, *S. aethiopica,* all biennials or short-lived perennials, are among the best. The large basal rosettes of silvery leaves are followed by tall spikes of flowers the second year. In clary sage, the flowers are upstaged by the large, colorful bracts, which persist long after the flowers have withered.

During visits to botanical gardens in recent years, I have seen a number of lovely sage species used in landscapes, including bog sage, *S. uliginosa;* the western native blue or Cleveland sage, *S. clevelandii;* forsythia salvia, the yellow *S. madrensis;* 'Purple Majesty', *S. guaranitica* × *gesneriflora;* rose-leaf, *S. involucrata;* and 'East Friesland', a cultivar from *S. nemorosa.*

I encourage you to experiment with different salvias each year to find new flower and bract colors and plant shapes for your garden. All of the sages with long tubular flowers attract and sustain hummingbirds, but none better than Texas sage, *Salvia coccinea,* a Gulf coastal plain perennial wildflower which grows as an annual elsewhere. I was surprised at the ability of dark violet-blue salvias such as *S. guaranitica* to draw hummingbirds. Even rose-leaf salvia, which has rather short, closely bunched, hooded, lavender-pink blossoms, drew the little ruby-throated hummers.

'Lady in Red,' an All-America Selections winner bred from the native American wildflower Salvia coccinea, attracts butterflies and hummingbirds. An annual, it is easily grown from seeds sown on warm soil.

Santolina spp.
Santolina or lavender cotton

Two species of santolina, the gray lavender cotton, *Santolina chamaecyparissus,* and green santolina, *S. virens,* are among the most popular

of herbs. Native to the dry, rocky soils of the Mediterranean area, they were used in ancient Roman gardens. The bitter-tasting, aromatic *S. chamaecyparissus* has medicinal properties but is mostly used now for edgings and in knot gardens, often alternated with the green species.

The leaves of santolina are a study in themselves. Although short and narrow, they are deeply cut. Densely clothing the fine ascending stems, they give santolina a frosted look. Young plants are round but continue to spread to make broad, foot-high mounds. In late summer, a heavy crop of rounded yellow puffball flowers about a half-inch in diameter rise above the foliage. In autumn, plants of santolina often fall open in the center and become rather messy-looking. At that time you can take tip cuttings from the vegetative branches and treat them as houseplants during the winter. On perfectly drained soil, santolina will live over winter in zone 5, but it should be cut back and mulched heavily further north.

Satureja spp.
Savory

You can see the relationship between *Satureja* and *satyr,* its root word, and probably could guess that savory was once used in love potions. More pragmatic people recognized its value for seasoning foods, particularly beans. Germanic people call it *bohnen kraut,* or bean herb.

The preferred savory for seasoning vegetables, potatoes, and meats is summer savory, *Satureja hortensis.* It has little landscape value, being a rather weak, lax plant with very slender, twisting branches and abundant but tiny purple flowers. Winter savory, *S. montana,* with mounded, densely leaved plants eight to ten inches high and tiny white flowers, makes a good landscape plant in groups of three or five. It is hardy through zone 4. The best landscaping savory, however, is dwarf winter savory, classified by some as *S. montana* 'Repens' and by others as *S. spicigera.* It is especially popular for edging herb beds, and makes neat little mounds no more than four inches high by a foot across.

The prettiest of all the savories is a native of the southeastern United States, Georgia savory, *Satureja ashei* × *georgiana*. It is a shrubby plant one to two feet high, hardy through zone 7. Grow it as an annual further north. The narrow leaves are highly aromatic and are used sparingly for imparting a minty flavor to cooked foods. The pink or lavender flowers are about a half-inch long and are borne over a long period. You may have to order this species from a nursery specializing in wildflowers.

Stachys byzantina
Lamb's ears

Hardly an herb garden anywhere is without lamb's ears. It is probably the most frequently planted silvery white herb in gardens and is used for edgings, groundcovers, and to intercede between wildly contrasting colors. Its long, woolly, silvery white leaves stay in good condition from spring through fall. It is very hardy, grows easily under daunting conditions, and spreads so robustly that it often looks a bit unkempt, but by pulling off a few blemished leaves you can shape it up. Lamb's ears stays low until its two-foot-high flower spikes shoot up; then it looks like a different plant. The common lamb's ears has insignificant flowers, but on the spikes of 'Silver Carpet' the lavender flowers are clearly visible.

The leaves of lamb's ears remain flexible when dry and are useful in crafts. The herb is hardy through the lower half of zone 5 without protection. You can usually get starts by asking around; lamb's ears are easy to propagate by digging rooted stems.

Tagetes lucida
Anise-scented marigold, rootbeer plant, winter tarragon

A half-hardy perennial, anise-scented marigold is grown as an annual in the North. It lived three years for me before succumbing, mostly because of my failure to divide the thick clumps. The erect plants grow one to two feet tall and have dark green, willowy foliage. They look good scattered here and there in herb gardens. The blossoms are like small, single yellow marigolds. They open just before frost in the South, but because they respond to lengthening nights, they open two or three weeks before frost in the North.

I know this herb well, having grown it for shipping as a substitute for French tarragon when the genuine article was dormant. (The chefs used it, but reluctantly, because it doesn't have the bite of French tarragon.) The plants don't look much like marigolds, but they are. Visitors to my garden seemed to like the powerful licorice fragrance of this plant more than that of any other on our herb farm. The leaves dry brittle but can add much to potpourris. Grow anise-scented marigold from tip cuttings or vegetative divisions; the seeds seldom mature before frost kills them.

Another marigold often seen in herb gardens is an old-timer sold under class names such as signet and gnome. It is *Tagetes tenuifolia,* and from it have come yellow and golden-orange varieties with tiny single flowers, no larger in diameter than a penny. Its foliage is finely cut and ferny, and somewhat grayer than the dark green foliage of French marigolds. The plants grow into broad mounds and bloom all summer except where heat is intense and unrelieved. The blossoms are often marketed as edible flowers. Grow it from seeds.

Tanacetum vulgare
Tansy

An ancient and honored herb, tansy has long enjoyed a reputation as a medicinal and strewing herb and has been used at burials. Its complex volatile oils contain several active medicinal and insect-repelling ingredients. I can't imagine bitter-flavored tansy being used to flavor foods, but it was centuries ago. Medicinal encyclopedias warn pregnant women not to ingest it.

Common tansy is native to Europe and perennial through zone 4; it grows to a height of three to four feet. My plants are quite tall and tend to flop after summer rains, but I support them unobtrusively with peony rings. The deeply cut foliage is attractive, but the tightly clustered yellow flowers are their most appealing feature.

For stunning clear green, finely cut foliage, grow the fern-leaved or *crispum* variety. Buy tansy plants or grow them from seeds or vegetative divisions.

A most unusual tansy, *T. ptarmicifolium* 'Silver Feather', has silvery white plants with twice-cut, feathery leaves. If you are tired of using dusty miller for silver accents, look for this. It grows from twelve to eighteen inches high, depending on the length of the season, and has small, flat clusters of typical tansy flowers in late summer. 'Silver Feather' will live over winter in zones 8 and 9 but is treated as an annual elsewhere. Grow it from seeds or cuttings; it may be hard to find.

Teucrium spp.
Germander, tree germander, cat thyme

Several hardy perennial teucriums are used in landscaping, along with a few tender species native to the Mediterranean area. By far the most familiar is the hardy, long-lived germander, *Teucrium chamaedrys.* You can keep it clipped for knot gardens or let it grow free into small, dark green subshrubs for edgings or groundcovers. Long grown for medicinal purposes, it is evergreen in zone 7 and south. Further north it freezes to the ground but will come back from the roots. The rose-pink flowers are borne over a long period beginning in early summer. A dwarf form, growing only four to six inches tall, is favored for groundcovers and miniature knot gardens.

Perhaps the most dramatic teucrium is the very white, tender, shrubby *T. fruticans,* or tree germander. I have seen it growing to about three feet in height at the National Herb Garden. Its medium blue axillary flowers are in startling contrast to the white tomentose leaves and stems. Cuttings can be taken in late summer for carrying through the winter as starts for the following year. Cat thyme, *T. marum,* similarly tender, looks a bit like tree germander but has smaller, more densely branched plants, and its purple flowers are carried in short spikes.

A lesser-known, pink-flowered, tender teucrium, *T. majoricum,* has pineapple-scented foliage and is a good plant for hanging baskets. Buy plants or start the teucriums from cuttings. Crowns of common germander also can be divided.

Thymus spp.
Thyme

You could carpet a space the size of a basketball court with one plant each of the different species and cultivars of thyme and still have plants left over. All would pass for landscaping; some are excellent; most are hardy through lower zone 4. Seed-grown common thyme is variable and is customarily grown as an annual in zone 4 and north. Most thymes are aromatic, but less than half the species are commonly used in seasonings and for medicinal purposes. Therefore, choosing thymes for your garden boils down first to deciding

Basil is the runaway favorite culinary herb. While common sweet basil is most often planted, herb gardeners like to add variety with recent introductions such as 'Green Ruffles' and 'Purple Ruffles'.

whether you want culinary thymes. Then you have to select the foliage colors or variegations, foliage textures, blossom colors, and particular flavors you like.

Most of the culinary thymes grow shrubby with age and assume a shape that is broader than tall. They don't carpet the ground as the low, spreading, purely ornamental thymes do. Among the culinary thymes, I like the low-growing green lemon thyme, *Thymus* × *citriodorus,* and the variegated golden lemon thyme. I have grown several types of common thyme and prefer the broad-leaved form of English thyme, a vegetatively propagated selection from *T. vulgaris.* While the creeping caraway thyme, *T. herba-barona,* has extremely fine leaves and wiry foliage and looks nondescript while green, it is extraordinarily beautiful when in bloom.

My favorites among the ornamental thymes are creeping red thyme, *T. pulegioides* 'Kermesinus'; woolly thyme, *T. pseudolanuginosus;* the glossy-leaved, lavender-flowered 'Dot Wells' thyme from *T. pulegiodes;* and a mat-forming green thyme that I have grown for years, variously referred to as *Thymus minus* or *T. minor.* If there are flowers, they are too small for me to see. Too, I am fond of common mother-of-thyme, *T. praecox* subsp. *arcticus,* in its many color forms. Although it has been four years since we closed our herb farm, a great old pink-flowered plant continues to spread on a sandy hillside, pushing back the weeds and grass. Of course, every time I visit a large herb garden when the thymes are in bloom, I come away smitten with a different cultivar.

No other landscaping plant can equal thyme for softening harsh lines and angles. You can tuck young thyme plants into the tiniest crevices in steps, between patio stones or bricks, and at the bases of large boulders and watch with delight as they unify disparate features. Common culinary thyme, *T. vulgaris,* and the various unimproved species reproduce true to seeds and are easy to grow. Look around the drip line of old plants of *T. vulgaris* and you will often find seedlings that can be potted up as replacements. Buy plants for the variegated thymes and cultivars selected for special foliage and blossom colors; they are vegetatively cloned to remain true to type. Grow common thyme from seeds or plants.

Appendix I:
Common and
Scientific Names

Appendix II:
Mail-Order Sources

Hardiness Zone Map

Acknowledgments

Photo Credits

Index

Common and Scientific Names

Scientific or botanical names are useful to herb enthusiasts because they provide the only precise, internationally recognized method for identifying plant genera, species, subspecies, and cultivars. Several kinds of plants may share a common name, but each has its own exclusive scientific name. Scientific names are basically in Latin, but since names of places and people can be "Latinized" and used to identify species, you may see names that seem to be English, German, French, Russian, Japanese, Chinese, and so on in derivation.

This book uses common names for herbs, but since some herb encyclopedias list scientific names first, we have prepared this cross-reference of kinds mentioned in the text or captions.

COMMON NAME(S)	CURRENT SCIENTIFIC NAME
Achillea or milfoil	*Achillea millefolium*
Agastache	*Agastache* species and hybrids
Angelica, common	*Angelica archangelica*
Angelica, Korean	*Angelica gigas*
Anise hyssop	*Agastache foeniculum*

COMMON NAME(S)	CURRENT SCIENTIFIC NAME
Anise-scented marigold, winter tarragon	*Tagetes lucida*
Arugula or roquette	*Eruca vesicaria* subsp. *sativa*
Autumn sage	*Salvia greggii* and hybrids
Basil, lemon	*Ocimum americanum*
Basil, sweet	*Ocimum basilicum* (includes most of the culinary basils)
Bay, bay laurel	*Laurus nobilis*
Bayberry, candleberry	*Myrica pensylvanica*
Beach wormwood, old woman	*Artemisia stellerana*
Bee balm, monarda, Oswego tea	*Monarda didyma, M. fistulosa,* and hybrids
Beefsteak, plant	*Perilla frutescens*
Benzoin	*Lindera benzoin*
Bergamot	*See* bee balm
Bistort	*Polygonum bistorta*
Black cumin, Roman coriander	*Nigella sativa*
Black mustard	*Brassica nigra*
Black peppermint	*Mentha* × *piperita*
Borage	*Borago officinalis*
Boxwood, dwarf English	*Buxus sempervirens* 'Suffruticosa'
Bugleweed	*Ajuga* species and hybrids
Calamint	*Calamintha* species and cultivars
Calendula, cape marigold	*Calendula officinalis*
Caper bush	*Capparis spinosa*
Caraway	*Carum carvi*
Caraway thyme	*Thymus herba-barona*
Carolina allspice	*Calycanthus florida*
Catmint	*Nepeta* species and cultivars
Catnip	*Nepeta cataria*
Cat thyme	*Teucrium marum*
Chamomile, Roman	*Chamaemelum nobile* (includes lawn chamomile 'Treneague')
Cherry-pie plant	*Heliotropum arborescens*
Chervil	*Anthriscus cerefolium*

Chili peppers or chilies	*Capsicum annuum*
Chives, common	*Allium schoenoprasum*
Chives, corkscrew or silver	*Allium senescens* 'Glaucum'
Chives, garlic	*Allium tuberosum*
Cilantro, coriander	*Coriandrum sativum*
Citrus geranium	*Pelargonium crispum*
Clary sage	*Salvia sclarea*
Comfrey, common	*Symphytum officinale*
Corsican mint, creme-de-menthe	*Mentha requienii*
Creeping thyme	Includes several *Thymus* species and cultivars, many from *T. praecox* subsp. *arcticus*
Cress, curled	*Lepidium sativum*
Cuban cilantro, culentro	*Eryngium foetidum*
Cuban oregano, Puerto Rican oregano	*Plectranthus amboinicus, P. a.* 'Variegatus', and *P. a.* 'Well-Sweep Wedgwood'
Culver's root	*Veronicastrum* virginicum
Curry plant	*Helichrysum angustifolium*
Cushionbush	*Calocephalus brownii*
Dame's rocket	*Hesperis matronalis*
Daylilies	*Hemerocallis* species and hybrids
Dill	*Anethum graveolens*
Dittany of Crete	*Origanum dictamnus*
Dusty miller	Includes species from *Senecio, Centaurea, Chrysanthemum, Tanacetum,* and *Artemisia*
English pennyroyal	*Mentha pulegium*
Epazote, Mexican tea, wormseed	*Chenopodium ambrosioides*
Ethiopian sage	*Salvia aethiopica*
False horehound	*Ballota acetabulosa*
False licorice	*Helichrysum petiolatum*
Fennel, Florence	*Foeniculum vulgare* var. *azoricum*
Fennel, sweet	*Foeniculum vulgare*
Feverfew	*Chrysanthemum parthenium*

COMMON NAME(S)	CURRENT SCIENTIFIC NAME
Florida anise, purple anise	*Illicium floridanum*
Foxglove, common	*Digitalis purpurea*
Foxglove, Grecian	*Digitalis lanata*
Garlic, common	*Allium sativum*
Garlic, serpent	*Allium sativum* var. *ophioscordon*
Georgia savory	*Satureja ashei* × *georgiana*
Germander	*Teucrium chamaedrys*
Giant hyssop	*Agastache mexicana*
Ginger, true	*Zingiber officinale*
Great blue lobelia	*Lobelia siphilitica*
Hops, common	*Humulus lupulus*
Horehound, common	*Marrubium vulgare*
Horehound, silver	*Marrubium incanum*
Horseradish	*Armoracia rusticana*
Hyssop	*Hyssopus officinalis*
Jerusalem oak, feather geranium	*Chenopodium botrys*
Jerusalem sage	*Phlomis fruticosa*
Johnny-jump-up	*Viola pedunculata, V. tricolor*
Lady's mantle, common	*Alchemilla* × *splendens*
Lamb's ears	*Stachys byzantina*
Laurel, bay laurel	*Laurus nobilis*
Lavender, English	*Lavandula angustifolia* (includes 'Munstead', 'Hidcote', 'Twickel Purple', 'Compacta Bomb', 'Short 'n' Sweet', and others)
Lavender, French or fringed	*Lavandula dentata*
Lavender cotton	*Santolina chamaecyparissus*
Lavandin, *Lavendula* × *intermedia*	Hybrids between *L. angustifolia* and *L. latifolia*
Lemon balm	*Melissa officinalis*
Lemon grass	*Cymbopogon citratus*
Lemon mint	*Monarda citriodora*
Lemon thyme	*Thymus* × *citriodorus*

Lemon verbena	*Aloysia triphylla*
Licorice, true	*Glycyrrhiza glabra*
Linden tree, European	*Tilia cordata*
Lovage	*Levisticum officinale*
Lungwort	*Pulmonaria officinalis*
Mache, corn salad	*Valerianella* species
Madder	*Rubia tinctorum*
Maltese cross	*Lychnis chalcedonica*
Marigold, signet or gem	*Tagetes tenuifolia*
Marsh mallow	*Althaea officinalis*
Mealycup sage	*Salvia farinacea*
Mexican bush salvia	*Salvia leucantha*
Mexican giant hyssop	*Agastache mexicana*
Mexican oregano	Many regional species; *Lippia graveolens* is best known
Mignonette	*Reseda odorata*
Milfoil	*See* achillea
Mother-of-thyme	*Thymus praecox* subsp. *arcticus*
Mountain mint	Several *Pycnanthemum* species
Mullein	*Verbascum thapsus* and others
Musk mallow	*Malva moschata*
Nasturtium	*Tropaeolum majus*
New Jersey tea	*Ceanothus americanus*
Nicotiana, evening-blooming jasmine tobacco	*Nicotiana alata*
Old man	*Artemisia abrotanum*
Orange bergamot mint	*Mentha aquatica* citrate form
Oregano, golden	*Origanum vulgare* subsp. *vulgare* 'Aureum'
Oregano, Greek	*Origanum vulgare* subsp. *hirtum*
Oregano, Italian	*Origanum* × *majoricum*
Oregano thyme	*Thymus pulegioides*
Orris or orris root	*Iris* × *germanica* var. *florentina*
Parsley	*Petroselinum crispum*
Pennyroyal, English	*Mentha pulegium*

COMMON NAME(S)	CURRENT SCIENTIFIC NAME
Pepper, ornamental	*Capsicum* species and hybrids
Peppermint	*Mentha* × *piperita*
Perilla	*Perilla frutescens*
Pineapple mint	*Mentha suaveolens* var. *variegata*
Pineapple sage	*Salvia elegans*
Pinks	*Dianthus* species and hybrids
Prairie coneflower	*Echinacea purpurea*
Rocambole	*Allium sativum* var. *ophioscordon*
Roman wormwood	*Artemisia pontica*
Rosemary	*Rosmarinus officinalis*
Roses, old	*Rosa* species and hybrids introduced prior to 1867
Rue	*Ruta graveolens*
Russian sage	*Perovskia atriplicifolia*
Safflower, false saffron	*Carthamus tinctorius*
Sage, garden	*Salvia officinalis* (includes several foliage colors and plant habits)
Salad burnet, burnet	*Poterium sanguisorba*
Santolina, gray; lavender cotton	*Santolina chamaecyparissus*
Santolina, green	*Santolina virens* or *S. ericoides*
Scented geranium	*Pelargonium* species and hybrids
Serpent garlic, rocambole	*Allium sativum* var. *ophioscordon*
Sesame, benne	*Sesamum indicum*
Shallots	*Allium cepa* var. *aggregatum*
Shiso, green perilla	*Perilla frutescens*
'Silver Feather'	*Tanacetum ptarmicifolium* 'Silver Feather'
Silver sage	*Salvia argentea*
Snakeweed	*Polygonum bistorta*
Society garlic	*Tulbaghia violacea*
Sorrel, garden or common	*Rumex acetosa*
Southernwood, old man	*Artemisia abrotanum*
Spanish lavender	*Lavandula stoechas*
Spearmint	*Mentha spicata*
Spotted lungwort	*Pulmonaria* species and hybrids

Summer savory	*Satureja hortensis*
Sweet cicely	*Myrrhis odorata*
Sweet marjoram	*Origanum majorana*
Sweet woodruff	*Galium odoratum*
Tansy, common and fern-leaved	*Tanacetum vulgare*
Tarragon, French tarragon	*Artemisia dracunculus* var. *sativa*
Teasel, Fuller's	*Dipsacus sativus*
Thrift	*Armeria maritima*
Thyme, common or French	*Thymus vulgaris*
Thyme, English	Includes several vegetatively propagated cultivars from *Thymus vulgaris*
Tree or silver germander	*Teucrium fruticans*
Tropical or Texas sage	*Salvia coccinea*
Vicks plant	*Plectranthus marrubioides, P. purpuratus, P. caerulus*
Viola	Many *Viola* species and hybrids
Wax myrtle	*Myrica cerifera*
Winter savory	*Satureja montana*
Woad	*Isatis tinctoria*
Woolly thyme	*Thymus pseudolanuginosus*
Woolly yarrow	*Achillea tomentosa*
Wormwood	*Artemisia* species and hybrids
Yarrow	*Achillea filipendula* and other species and hybrids

Appendix II

Mail-Order
Sources

There may come a time in your life when you can't find the herb cultivars you want in your local garden center or in the catalogs of major mail-order seed and plant companies. Then you can send for a catalog from one or more of the many small to medium-size mail-order nurseries specializing in plants and/or seeds of herbs.

The descriptions of herbs in most catalogs are quite brief, but they are usually sufficient to help you choose between the different cultivars or varieties of a given species. Some producers offer only price lists, which give cultivar names and prices but no descriptions.

Catalogs don't always agree on botanical names; some cling to obsolete nomenclature and others use names that are more generic than scientific. This muddled situation is only partly the fault of seed and plant marketers; the North American herb industry has only recently benefited from the services of plant taxonomists who are qualified to sort through and accurately name the confusing mass of herb genera and species and to begin to identify the cultivars that are being sold under two or more names.

I would advise that whenever you can, visit your chosen herb specialist rather than order by mail. Most of the sources listed below operate retail shops or greenhouses, and you may be able to buy larger plants than are customarily shipped by mail. Herb specialists enjoy sharing their love for herbs and will fill your head with good information while filling your car trunk with plants. Send for a catalog and check their business hours before setting out. The prices listed for catalogs are for the year of publication of this book. Some nurseries apply the cost of the catalog against your first order. Be sure to send a letter-size self-addressed stamped envelope (SASE) if asked, or your request for a price list or catalog may not be honored.

Gardeners in the deep South and warm West who need plants very early in the spring should order from growers in their climate zones. Northern growers are reluctant to ship during extremely cold weather for fear of damage to the tender, greenhouse-grown herbs en route.

The sources are listed by region.

NEW ENGLAND AND MID-ATLANTIC STATES

Cricket Hill Herb Farm, Ltd.
Glen St.
Rowley, MA 01969
Catalog $1, not refunded

Fox Hollow Herbs
P.O. Box 148
McGrann, PA 16236
Catalog $1, not refunded

Glade Valley Nursery
9226 Links Rd.
Walkersville, MD 21793
Herbs and scented geraniums.
No charge for price list

Hartman's Herb Farm
1026 Old Dana Road
Barre, MA 01005
Catalog $2, refunded with first order

The Herb Barn
H.C. 64, Box 435D
Trout Run, PA 17771
Send $.50 or SASE for price list

Kingfisher, Inc.
(Halcyon Garden Products)
P.O. Box 75
Wexford, PA 15090
Catalog and guide to growing herbs,
$2, not refunded

Logee's Greenhouses
141 North St.
Danielson, CT 06239
Herbs, houseplants, and perennials.
Catalog $3, refunded with first order

Maryland's Herb Basket
Box 131
Millington, MD 21651
Catalog $1, not refunded

The Rosemary House
120 S. Market St.
Mechanicsburg, PA 17055
Catalog $3, not refunded

Tinmouth Channel Farm
RR 1, Box 428B
Tinmouth, VT 05773
Catalog $2, not refunded

Triple Oaks Nursery
Rt. 47
Franklinville, NJ 08322
Price list, no charge. Must send SASE

Well-Sweep Herb Farm
317 Mt. Bethel Rd.
Port Murray, NJ 07865
Catalog $2, not refunded

Wrenwood of Berkeley Springs
Rt. 4, Box 361
Berkeley Springs, WV 25411
Herbs and perennials. Catalog $2, not refunded

SOUTH AND SOUTHEAST

Bo's Nursery
12743 Gillard Rd.
Winter Garden, FL 34787
Price list, no charge; booklet of descriptions, planting care, and recipes, $2, refunded with first order

Good Hollow Greenhouse & Herbarium
50 Slate Rock Mill Road
Taft, TN 38488
Price list, no charge. Send SASE

McCrory's Sunny Hill Herb Farm
35152 LaPlace Court
Eustis, FL 32726
Price list $.50, refunded with first order

Rasland Farm
NC 82 at US 13
Godwin, NC 28344-9712
Catalog $3, not refunded

Sandy Mush Herb Nursery
Rt. 2, Surrett Cove Rd.
Leicester, NC 28748
Herb handbook/catalog $4, not refunded

Rose Hill Herbs & Perennials
Rt. 4, Box 377
Amherst, VA 24521
Catalog $2

Southern Seeds
P.O. Box 2091
Melbourne, FL 32902
Catalog $1, not refunded

Village Arbors
1804 Saugahatchee Rd.
Auburn, AL 36830
Catalog $1

MIDWEST

Alyce's Herbs
P.O. Box 9563
Madison, WI 53715
Catalog $1

Companion Plants
7247 North Coolville Ridge Rd.
Athens, OH 45701
Catalog $2, not refunded

The Farmhouse
10,000 N.W. 70th St.
Grimes, IA 50111
Catalog $1, not refunded

The Gathered Herb & Greenhouse
12114 N. State Rd.
Otisville, MI 48463
Catalog $2, refunded with first order

The Herb Barn
1955 Greenley Ave.
Benton Harbor, MI 49022
Seeds only. Catalog $1, refunded with first order

Herbs-Liscious
1702 S. 6th St.
Marshalltown, IA 50158
Catalog $2, refunded with first order

Lily of the Valley Herb Farm
3969 Fox Ave.
Minerva, OH 44657
Plant price list $1, product price list $1, refunded with first orders

Shady Hill Gardens
831 Walnut St.
Batavia, IL 60510
Scented geraniums. Catalog $2, refunded with first order

GREAT PLAINS AND ROCKY MOUNTAIN STATES

The Gourmet Gardener
4000 West 126th Street
Leawood, KS 66209
Catalog $2

Rabbit Shadow Farm
2880 East Highway 402
Loveland, CO 80537
Herb topiaries and scented geraniums. Catalog $1, not refunded

TEXAS AND SOUTHWEST

Hilltop Herb Farm
at Chain O' Lakes Resort
P.O. Box 325
Romayor, TX 77368
Price list free, must include SASE

CALIFORNIA

Heirloom Garden Seeds
P.O. Box 138
Guerneville, CA 95446
Catalog $3

Shepherd's Garden Seeds
6116 Highway 9
Felton, CA 95018
Catalog $1, not refunded; sent first-class mail

Taylor's Herb Gardens
1535 Lone Oak Road
Vista, CA 92084
Catalog $3, not refunded

NORTHWEST

Dutch Mill Herb Farm
Rt. 2, Box 190
Forest Grove, OR 97116
Lavender specialist. Price list only, free; send letter-size SASE

Goodwin Creek Gardens
P.O. Box 83
Williams, OR 97544
Catalog $1, not refunded

Seeds Blum
Idaho City Stage
Boise, ID 83706
Catalog $3, not refunded

CANADA AND AUSTRALIA

Dacha Barinka
25232 Strathcona Rd.
Chilliwack, British Columbia
Canada V2P 3AT2
Catalog $1, refunded with first order

Kings Herb Seeds
P.O. Box 975
Penrith, New South Wales
Australia 2751
Because exchange rates fluctuate, check with this company before ordering a catalog. At the time this source list was compiled, the catalog cost about $14 US, largely because of the cost of airmail.

Rawlinson Garden Seed
269 College Road
Truro, Nova Scotia
Canada B2N 2P6
Catalog free within Canada; $1 to U.S. customers, refunded with first $10 order; $1.50 overseas, refunded with first $15 order

Richters
357 Highway 47
Goodwood, Ontario
Canada LOC 1AO
Seed and plant catalog $2 to North America, $4 elsewhere

Tregunno Seeds
c/o Ontario Seed Co., Ltd.
P.O. Box 144, 16 King St. South
Waterloo, Ontario
Canada N2J 3Z9
Catalog free

NOTE: I have made every attempt to verify the completeness and accuracy of this listing. All companies who advertise were contacted and given the opportunity to check the information. I have not listed companies specializing in dried herbs and supplies for herb crafts. Gardeners who live outside of North America should check before ordering a catalog, as the cost may be higher than listed because of postage.

USDA Hardiness Zone Map

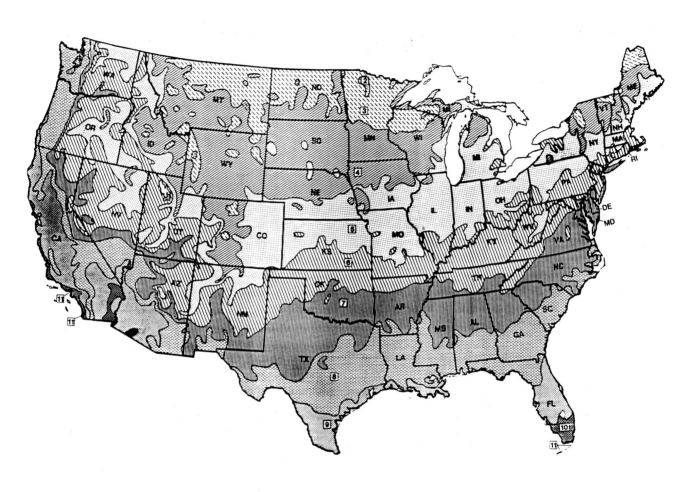

Range of Average Annual Minimum
Temperatures for Each Zone

ZONE 1	BELOW −50°F
ZONE 2	−50° TO −40°
ZONE 3	−40° TO −30°
ZONE 4	−30° TO −20°
ZONE 5	−20° TO −10°
ZONE 6	−10° TO 0°
ZONE 7	0° TO 10°
ZONE 8	10° TO 20°
ZONE 9	20° TO 30°
ZONE 10	30° TO 40°
ZONE 11	ABOVE 40°

Acknowledgments

Special thanks to my fellow garden writer Rosalie Davis, of Jamaica Plain, Massachusetts, for her creative ideas on employing herbs in landscapes in northern climates. Thanks, too, to Arthur O. Tucker, Ph.D., Delaware State College, for a great deal of data on modern nomenclature; Tom DeBaggio, T. DeBaggio Herbs, Arlington, Virginia; Holly Shimizu, U.S. Botanic Garden; Fairman and Kate Jane, Sandy Mush Herb Nursery, Leicester, North Carolina; Janet Walker, National Herb Garden; Mary Ellen and Ervin Ross, Merry Gardens, Camden, Maine; Barbara Remington, Dutch Mill Herb Farm, Forest Grove, Oregon; Jim and Theresa Mieseler, Shady Acres Herb Farm, Chaska, Minnesota (especially for hardiness data); Judith Kehs, Cricket Hill Herb Farm, Ltd., Rowley, Massachusetts; Tillie Bohannon, Bo's Nursery, Winter Garden, Florida (for summer survival data); Ellie Donley, Western Reserve Herb Garden, Cleveland, Ohio; Joy Logee Martin and Tovah Martin, Logee's Greenhouses, Danielson, Connecticut; Louise and Cyrus Hyde, Well-Sweep Herb Farm, Port Murray, New Jersey; and Otto Richter, Richter's, Goodwood, Ontario, Canada. (If I've missed anyone who helped, I owe you one!)

I used *Hortus Third* as a reference for scientific names except when nomenclature has changed since its publication. The encyclopedic reference *Herbs,* by Roger Phillips and Nicky Foy, provided useful information on herbs that are popular in Europe but little known in North America.

Photo Credits

Cathy Wilkinson Barash, xx–1, 150, 157; Nancy Beaubaire, 78–79, 84–85; Roger Bickel, viii, xvi–xvii, xvii, 125; Rita Buchanan, 23, 39, 91, 94, 95, 99, 102, 109, 120–121, 122; Karen Bussolini, 10–11, 17, 30–31, 34, 42, 51, 56, 58, 65, 66–67, 98, 127, 147, 165; Lois Chaplin, 152; Rosalind Creasy, xiii, 4–5, 28, 47, 55, 72 *bottom,* 77, 93; Page Dickey, 9; Thomas Eltzroth, 40–41, 48; Derek Fell, 118, 128–129, 131, 132; Bettie Furuta, 83; Kristi Jones, 8, 24–25, 69, 90–91; Dency Kane, iv–v, x–xi, xix, 74–75, 96–97, 158, 166, 183; Judy Kehs, 104–105; David Morris, 36–37; Diana Petrauskas, 2, 7, 16, 18–19, 33, 35, 72 *top,* 171, 176–177; Holly Shimizu, 52–53, 181 *top;* George Taloumis, 27, 44–45, 110, 158–159, 188; Jim Wilson, 14, 21, 22, 45, 57, 62, 88 *top and bottom,* 114, 115, 129, 134–135, 138, 141, 181 *bottom.*

Index

Absinthe, 143
Absorbents, 89
Achillea (yarrow), 132, 135–36. *See also*
    Yarrow
  'Gold Plate', 12, 15, 136
  'Moonshine', 15
Achillea millefolium (milfoil), 64, 136, *166,*
    167
Achillea tomentosa (woolly yarrow), *7, 38,*
    136, *176–77*
Agastache (giant hyssop), 6, 136–37
Agastache cana (mosquito plant), 137
Agastache coccinea 'Firebird', 34
Agastache foeniculum (anise hyssop), 136–37.
    See also Anise hyssop
Agastache mexicana (Mexican giant hyssop),
    26, 29, 137
Agastache rugosa (Korean mint), 137
Alchemilla (lady's mantle), 3, 9, 13, 16, 50,
    107, 118, 137–38
Alexanders, 113
Allium (chives), 50, 128, *129,* 139. *See also*
    Chives
Allium sativum var. *ophioscorodon*
    (rocambole or serpent garlic),
    70, 139–40
Allium schoenoprasum (common chives), 9,
    15, 139, *176–77*
Allium senescens (silver or corkscrew
    chives), 32, 139, 170, *171*
Allium tuberosum (garlic chives), xii, *xiii,* 15,
    39, 71, 125, *129, 134–35,* 139
Allspice, Carolina, 26
Aloysia triphylla (lemon verbena), 140. *See*
    also Lemon verbena
Althea, 71
Alyssum, sweet, *18–19, 28, 51,* 60, 86, 92, *93*
Angelica (angelica), 12, 16, *44–45,* 73, 113,
    140, 142
  Korean, 12, 13, 38, 142
Angelica archangelica, 142

Angelica gigas (Korean angelica), 12, 13, 38,
    142
Anise, 113
Anise hyssop, 29, 32, 136–37
  in arrangement, *129*
  and containers, 81
  division of, 116
  as fragrant, 3
  harvesting of, 126
  and paved area, 63
  seeding of, 113
  and walls, 60
Anise-scented basil, 23, 29, 164, 167
Anise-scented marigold, 13, 29, 51, 113,
    126, *181,* 185–86
Armeria maritima (thrift), 46
Aromatic herbs, 71, 76. *See also* Fragrance
Artemisia (wormwood), 142–43. *See also*
    Wormwood
Artemisia abrotanum (old man), 143
  'Tangerine', 143
Artemisia dracunculus var. *sativa* (French
    tarragon), 116, 118, 124, 143
Artemisia ludoviciana, 143
Artemesias, 143
  as border, 6, 9
  at Caprilands Herb Farm, xii, *xiii*
  dwarf, 60
  as edging herb, 170, 171
  'Lambrook Silver', 143
  'Powys Castle', 142
  'Silver Brocade', 38, 142–43
  'Silver King', *35, 36–37, 44–45,* 143
  'Silver Mound', 34, 51, 142, 143, 170, 171,
    172
  'Silver Queen', 143
  and stones, 64
  and wreath-making, 73
Artemisia schmidtiana, 142
Artemisia stellerana (beach wormwood),
    142–43

Hummingbirds, 19, 28, 61, 162, 182
Humulus (hop, hop vine), 153
    'Aureus', 153
Humulus japonicus (Japanese hops), 153
Humulus lupulus (European hops), 153
Hyssop, 2, 3, 13, 23, 32, 76, 113, 153–54
    anise, 29, 32, 136–37 (*see also* Anise
        hyssop)
    giant, 136–37
    Mexican giant, 26, 29, 137
    'Rubrum', 50–51
Hyssopus officinalis (hyssop), 50, 153–54

Indoor growing of herbs, 117–19
Inniswood Metro Gardens (Ohio), 134–35
Insects, 112
Iris, 76
    Florentine, 6, 60
Irrigation system, 108
Isatis tinctoria (woad), 73

Jasmine tobacco, 29
Jerusalem sage, 38, 60, 173
Johnny-jump-up, 16, 61, 86

Kitchen garden herb culture, 67–70, 73–76
Knot gardens, 1, 43, *157*, 180, 184, 187
Koir (coconut fiber), 81
Korean angelica, 12, 13, 38, 142
Korean mint, 137

Lady's mantle, 3, 9, 13, 16, 50, 107, *118*,
    137–38
Lamb's ears, 15, 32, *36–37, 39, 45, 51*, 185
Landscaping, with containers of herbs, 82–
    86
Laurus nobilis (bay), 154–55
Lavender, xii, *24–25, 28, 30–31*, 32, *36–37,
    39*, 155–56, 165
    in arrangement, *129*
    as border, 3, 6, 9, 12, 17
    from cuttings, 116
    as decorative, 71
    as edging herb, *42*, 43, 46, *48*
    as fragrant, 15, 20, *21, 66–67*, 71
    harvesting of, 126, *128, 129*
    in kitchen garden, 68, 69
    in linen closet, 133
    in Mediterranean theme, 76
    in Middle Ages theme, 76
    overwintering of, 119
    and paved area, 54
    at Peconic River Herb Farm, 74–75
    in planter box, 90–91

in raised bed, 10–11
as seedlings, 113
and stonework, 53, 59, 60
and sun, 23, 61
varieties
    'Compacta Bomb', 46
    English, *84–85*, 155
    fringed, 92
    'Hidcote', *18–19*, 155
    'Montana Blizzard', 155
    'Munstead', 155, 156
    'Short 'n' Sweet', 46
    'Twickel', 46
    'Twickel Purple', 15, 155
Lavender cotton, 73, 182, 184
    gray, 8
Lavandin, 155–56
Lavandula (lavender, lavandin), 155–56
Lavandula angustifolia, 155–56
Lavandula × *intermedia* (lavandin), 155–56
Lavandula latifolia, 155
Lavandula spica, 155
Lavandula vera, 155
Lemon balm, 160–61
    and containers, 79
    as culinary herb, 123
    as edging herb, 46, 47
    foliage of, 13
    fragrance of, 26
    in kitchen garden, 73
    in path, 20
    and paving patterns, 63
    in planter box, *90–91*
    and sun or shade, 16, 61
Lemon basil, 13, 23, 26, 49, 164
Lemon grass, 29, 63, 70, 73, 92
Lemon marigold, 78–79
Lemon mint, 162, 163
Lemon-scented peppermint, 29
Lemon-scented thyme, 26, 59
Lemon thyme, 50, 123
Lemon verbena, 26, 140
    as border, 3, 12, 13
    and container, 81
    cuttings of, 116
    harvesting of, 126
    in hedges, 50
    overwintering of, 92
    and paving patterns, 63
    as tea herb, 71
Lettuce, romaine, *84–85*
Licorice, 29, 46, *47*
    false, 6, 26, 82, 88, 151, 153
Licorice basil, 29